Cheeper

Written & Illustrated by

Sarah E. Brown

Cheeper

Cheeper

Cover design by Sarah E. Brown.

ISBN-13: 978-0692466803 (Sarah E. Brown)

ISBN-10: 0692466800

Cover painting copyright © 2014 by Sarah E. Brown.

Illustrations copyright © 2014 by Sarah E. Brown.

Unless otherwise stated, all references are taken from the *New Living Translation*, used with permission.

Cheeper is based on a true event. Cheeper the robin, the Brown family, and the events that took place while the two were in contact have been depicted as accurately as possible. The events that are portrayed as happening after Cheeper left the Brown family are based on the author's imagination and habits of robins in general.

For more information about the habits and characteristics of the American Robin, see http://www.learner.org/jnorth/robin as well as http://www.allaboutbirds.org/guide/American_Robin.

For more about the author see http://www.sarahellenbrown.com.

To connect with the author and receive updates about future works, writing tips, and illustration ideas, see http://facebook.com/sarahbrownauthor.

Dedicated to Cheeper…

wherever he is!

In memory of Aleicia Ann.

2008

Cheeper

A photograph of Cheeper sitting in my hand
soon after his real feathers came in.

Table of Contents

Introduction

Cheeper came into our family's lives in 2011, after a June wind storm brought down the tree that housed his nest. He was a joy to raise, this cocky little robin of ours. All the facts about his life while with our family are accurately told in this story. As recounted in the chapter titled "Change," there came point after a month or two when Cheeper became so acclimated to his life outdoors that he no longer came to us when we called him. We sometimes heard him answering our calls from various places in the yard, and once we saw him with another robin in the bushes across the road.

From that point on, I took the story in hand and used my imagination and facts that I learned from researching the habits of robins to weave the adventures of Cheeper's life. We like to think that he lived and thrived, flew south for the winter, returned home in the spring, and found a mate and raised a family. Perhaps one of the many sleek, healthy robins we've seen hunting worms in our yard is Cheeper or one of his children. Although there's no way to be certain, it could be, since robins are known to return to their birthplaces year after year.

There are three basic themes throughout this book:

1. Seasons. It is only in death that new life can arise.
2. Sorrow. It is often in sorrow that deeper joy is found.
3. Song. "Ask the birds… and they will tell you" (Job 12:7).

Allow me to expound:

1. Seasons. Nature is one of God's revelations of Himself, another being His Word. There is clear evidence for God in the world around us (Psalm 19:1; Acts 14:17; Romans 1:20). God's love is manifested in nature in His care and compassion for even the smallest of creatures. In the seasons— summer, autumn, winter, and spring—can be seen an object lesson of God's plan of salvation. The seasons show that it is only in death that new life can arise. "Unless a kernel of wheat is planted in the soil and dies, it remains alone. But its death will

produce many new kernels—a plentiful harvest of new lives" (John 12:24, KJV). Just as the leaves die and fall to the ground in autumn, and the new grasses rise and new leaves sprout in the spring, so Christ willingly laid down His life and rose again to pay the price for our sins. Because of His sacrifice, we can have the power to die to self and rise again to new life in Him. One of my favorite authors put it this way:

> "The trees cast off their leaves, only to be robed with fresher [greenness]; the flowers die, to spring forth in new beauty; and in every manifestation of creative power is held out the assurance that we may be created new in 'righteousness and holiness of truth.' Ephesians 4:24."[1]

2. Sorrow. If God loves us and cares about us, then why do we experience pain and sorrow? Suffering is a part of life. We do not live in a perfect world anymore. Since the onset of sin, the whole creation has been subjected to degeneration and pain. While

---

[1] White, E. G. (1903). *Education.* Mountain View, CA: Pacific Press Publishing Association.

no one would wish to experience hardship and heartache in life, neither should anyone wish for a life of ease. Why? Because deeper joy is found through sorrow. When life is easy and carefree, people tend to take their blessings for granted. They tend to become selfish and feel entitled. Sorrow has a way of showing humanity its need of God. If someone turns to Him in sorrow, rather than letting the pain harden their heart, that sorrow will produce lasting joy. Suddenly, that person begins to anticipate and appreciate the little bits of beauty and pleasure that are granted him or her.

3. Song. "Ask the birds of the sky, and they will tell you" (Job 12:7). The passage goes on to say that the birds will declare the works of the Lord. I believe that if the birds could speak our language, they would wholeheartedly acknowledge the existence of the Creator. I believe that their songs are songs of praise to God. But a God of love? That could be a new concept. Cheeper was a very unique bird, having been raised in our home and exposed to our faith in a God of love. In my story, I speculate that, not having parents to teach him the songs of the robins, Cheeper finds himself unable to sing from his heart.

He comes to understand that heartfelt songs of praise to a loving God cannot come from one whose life had been ever pleasant and happy and rosy, but only from a heart that has gone through trials and anguish without losing hope—a heart that can find beauty in the midst of pain, and joy in spite of sadness.

I hope you enjoy this story, but more than this, I hope it speaks the messages of God's love and care *for you* into your heart, thus enabling you to truly love and serve those around you.

Part I
Summer

<u>Storm</u>

A mother robin glided through the air above a dusty gravel road, a fat worm dangling from her yellow beak. Shimmering rays of late afternoon sunshine beat down on her back. An occasional gust of sweltering air stirred the tall grasses alongside the road and tried to push her off course.

The sun was shifting westward on the hazy horizon, and stately trees were beginning to cast shadows on a blue house on top of a hill near the road. The winding road did not end at the house, however. If the mother robin had desired to follow its course, she would have crossed a meandering creek, passed a corn field, and sailed by a few more houses before it trailed off into a bumpy field road.

This mother robin was on a mission, though, not out for casual sightseeing. Her sharp eyes could detect a slight movement not far away in a tree above the creek. There the piercing sunlight filtered through the leaves and rested upon a nest of sticks and mud built snugly into the fork of two branches. Inside the nest, a small, naked bird, not more than a week old, had laid his head back and opened his beak as wide as he could in anticipation of the juicy meal that would soon be dropped down his throat.

The mother robin circled the tree, cautiously glancing about to make sure no hawks or eagles were nearby to spy out the location of the nest with its precious cargo. There was another baby in the nest, just as pink and naked as the first, but he was contentedly waiting for his food—unlike his hungry brother, who continued his silent plea.

Assured that all was safe, Mother Robin fluttered down to rest on a nearby branch. Instantly the two little heads popped up—each beak opening as wide as possible. Though still as blind as at birth, they knew who the fluttering had come from. Both begged to be the first to receive whatever their mother had brought.

The red-breasted mother robin hesitated for a moment above the nest, unsure which of her demanding offspring to serve the morsel to. She finally gave up trying to decide and shoved the worm down the throat of the nearest squirming baby, who swallowed the large mouthful in one frantic gulp. His hunger finally satisfied, the little

baby robin settled down quietly beside his brother in the nest.

Soon another form alighted on the edge of the nest and tucked a bug into the gaping mouth of the other youngster. Father and Mother Robin, who had been finding and fetching food for their family all afternoon, hopped wearily onto a higher branch. The mother softly began to sing a sweet song of thanksgiving to the Creator.

In the nest below, the little ones' heads began to nod as they drifted into dreamland. The mother robin's singing revived her tired spirits, and she trilled each tune with greater gusto than the last. Soon the father robin joined in, and the two sang a lilting lullaby in beautiful harmony to their slumbering children.

Abruptly they stopped. The valley had suddenly been plunged into eerie shadows. A bank of dark, angry clouds was snaking its way across the sky, hiding the sun from view. The humidity was becoming increasingly oppressive, and the air held an ominous feeling.

Mother Robin peered anxiously through the leaves at the approaching storm, and Father Robin cast a worried glance at the babies in the nest. In the distance, a streak of lightning stabbed at the earth and an angry rumble of thunder shook the air.

Splat, splat, splat. The first large raindrops made tiny craters in the dusty gravel road. More raindrops followed, faster and faster until a torrent of rain broke loose over the valley, pelting the blue house, the dusty road, and the nest in the tree with huge, cold drops. Mother Robin raced to the nest and hurried to fluff her warm wings over her babies.

Safe and warm in the dark hollow of the nest under their brave mother, the baby robins listened to the sounds of the storm that raged outside. They could hear the rushing rain, the booming thunder, and the howling wind, but the nest had been well built and did not leak a drop.

The branch began to sway as the wind blew stronger and stronger. Mother Robin bent her head to its blasts and clung tightly to the sides of the nest. Father Robin hung on a

tossing branch overhead, keeping his balance and hovering protectively over his family. They had been through storms before, and they usually passed just as quickly as they had come.

This time, however, the storm seemed to be possessed with strangely wicked intentions—a frightening fury that drove it on and on. The wind rose from a howl to a shriek, and all the occupants of the nest could hear the tree groaning under its pressure. The air became thick with twigs and leaves that the wind had torn from other trees.

A sickening cracking noise exploded from the tree. They were falling—*falling*—as the tree broke under the strain of the wind. With frightened squawks, Mother and Father Robin took flight and rose above the falling limbs, where the currents of racing wind pulled them far from the scene.

An instant later the tree hit the ground with a crash and the baby robins were thrown from the safety of the nest. Before he even knew what was happening to him, the persistent brother robin hit the muddy gravel with a force that knocked the breath out of him. Everything blackened for a moment. He lay there gasping.

Cold rain washed over him, reviving him slightly. Slushy balls of icy hail fell all around him, and the shrieking wind stabbed his naked body with cold. Every few seconds the baby robin heard another sickening *crack*, sometimes close and sometimes far away, and twigs and branches thudded to the ground all around him.

He faded in and out of consciousness. How long had he lain in the rubble of the fallen tree being washed by the floods of rain? Was it only minutes? Or hours? Or maybe days! His body numbed with the cold, and he ceased to hear the ferocious storm that raged around him. Instead, thoughts of warm sunshine dancing on the nest filled his mind… and then everything went blank.

Rescue

Strange voices finally brought the little robin back to consciousness. For a minute he did not know where he was or what had happened. Why wasn't he in the nest? Where was his mother? Why did his body feel stiff with icy numbness?

Then it all came rushing back to him—the storm, the wind, the falling tree, the hail. He tried to move, but he ached so badly that he gave up and lay limply sprawled on the muddy gravel. Everything was now still, except for a soft breeze that whispered in the leaves overhead. The tempest had finally vented its anger and passed on.

The voices cut through the calm of the evening. The little robin listened closely as they came nearer and nearer. Boots sloshed through mud puddles and crunched on the gravel road, and exclamations of amazement and horror were uttered.

"Look at all the branches the wind blew down!" a girl cried. The baby robin heard the snapping of twigs and the rustling of leaves as whoever it was stepped over a large limb obstructing the path.

"Dad says there are over fifteen trees down in the woods behind the house!" a woman's voice exclaimed.

"Oh, Mom, look!" the first voice called. "The tree by the creek is down and blocking the road!" The footsteps approached where the robin lay.

The blind baby robin lay listening as he heard the mother stoop and pick something up. "Look, Sarah!" she called to her daughter. "I found a nest lying here! It's empty, though, so maybe no birds were using it when the tree came down."

Cheeper

The robin heard Sarah hurry over to examine the empty nest of sticks and mud that her mother held. Unexpectedly she cried out, "Mom, what's that?" And then the footsteps approached him, stopping by his side. His little heart beat swiftly, but he was so cold and stunned that he couldn't move.

"Why, it's a baby birdie!" Mom bent down to take a closer look.

"Is he dead?" Sarah's voice was filled with pity.

Warm hands eased under the little robin's cold, stiff body and lifted him from the ground. "His heart is still beating! I can't believe he didn't get killed when the tree fell!"

"What do we do?" Sarah's voice was full of wonder.

Mom's voice was ever practical, "His mother isn't around and he'll die if we leave him here, so I guess we'd better take him inside and try to revive him."

"Oh, look, Mom! There's another one!" Sarah cried again. The baby robin felt movement as his carrier bent to look at what her daughter had pointed out. What were they looking at?

"I don't think this one's alive." Mom's sad words sounded very far away as another wave of dazed sleepiness began to envelope the robin in her hands. Words like

20

"broken neck," "dead birdie," and "bury" all jumbled together in incomprehensible echoes.

Movement again brought him back to reality. The warm hands were still cupped around him, and he was being tucked into something warm and soft. His head spun and his ears rang and he felt oh-so-cold. The person was carrying him somewhere. He probably should have been frightened, but he was just so glad to be off the cold, hard ground and in the security of the soft cloth that at the moment he didn't care what his future held. The sounds faded as he again slipped into unconsciousness.

Darkness

The little robin stirred. Oh, he was so warm and cozy! Surely he was back in his nest on a sunny day. Perhaps the terrible storm had just been a dream. He must be cuddled back beside his brother with his mother or father's soft breast covering him. But no, the fluffy cloth that he was tucked into didn't feel quite like the downy feathers lining the nest in the tree.

The robin began to awaken more fully. He couldn't hear the creek trickling down below, or the wind playing with the leaves overhead, or the twittering of birds, or any of the sounds that he knew he should have heard if he was in the nest. So where was he?

Well, wherever he was, it was certainly warm and toasty. The baby robin stretched his wings and yawned. His limbs no longer tingled with cold, and he felt almost as good as new, except for his hungry tummy. He tilted his head back and opened his beak wide. Perhaps one of his parents was nearby with a crunchy bug or juicy worm to pop in his mouth.

"Mom, come and see!" The voice of the girl startled the robin. "Quickly, Mom," she excitedly called again. "The baby robin is awake!"

"Oh, praise the Lord!" The robin heard Mom's voice and approaching footsteps. "See, Sarah, he just needed to be warmed up."

"He seems to like the little box that we lined with flannel; he's all snuggled into it."

The box was wonderful. The empty stomach was a little harder to enjoy.

"Look, Sarah, he must be hungry. He's opening his mouth and waiting for food."

"I wonder what we should feed him," the robin heard Sarah ask. "He'd probably eat bugs or spiders, but I don't know if we could catch enough."

Bugs and spiders sounded delicious, but these people would be flying around all day long if they wanted to keep his hunger satisfied on such small creatures.

"Well," Mom mused, "if he *is* a baby robin, I guess the best food for him is earthworms."

"From the garden?"

Cheeper

"Sure! It wouldn't be too hard to dig up some every day. Run and find a container to put the worms in, and I'll go get the shovel."

A lot of clattering and clamoring followed. Footsteps and unrecognizable thumps and bangs resounded. Then one final bang and all was quiet. The baby robin could finally hear himself think again. His rescuers must have carried out Mom's orders and flown off in search of earthworms. Or *had* they flown? Now that he thought about it, the robin couldn't remember ever hearing the flapping of wings. These humans must not use their wings very often—unless, perhaps they did not have any.

Not long after, Mom and Sarah returned from the garden, and the silence was broken. The robin felt himself being lifted out of his box. "Here, Sarah," Mom instructed, "wash the dirt off one of these earthworms and we'll put it in his mouth to see if he swallows it."

Gentle fingers opened the robin's mouth and a cold, clammy worm was dropped inside. In an instant, he gobbled it down and opened his beak wide to beg for more.

"He really is hungry!" Sarah laughed. "Just see how fast the worms disappear!" She dropped another worm down the expectant robin's throat. "You know, Mom, I was so worried he was going to die when we first brought him inside. He was so droopy and didn't respond to our touches

24

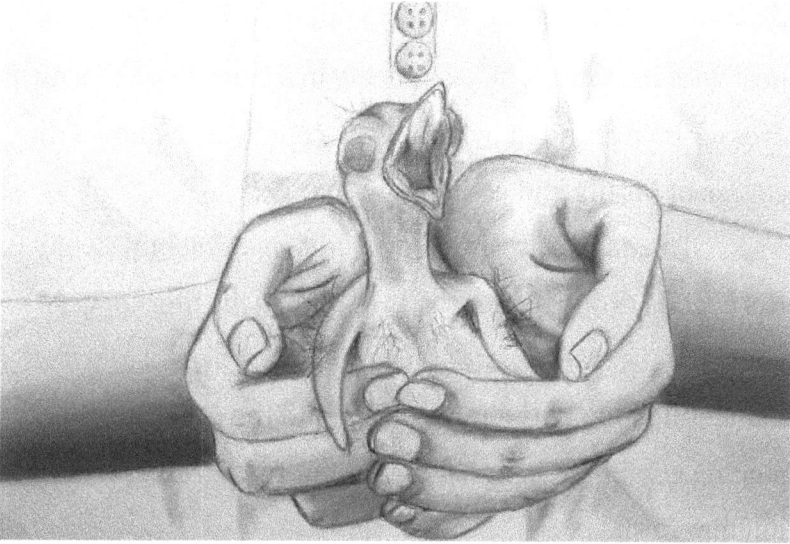

or anything. But I was praying that he would revive, and just see how perky he looks now!"

Mom's voice was quiet. "I was praying too, Sarah. It's a miracle that he didn't die when the tree came down."

"And it's a good thing that we went outside when we did, or we might have been too late to rescue him," Sarah added.

As he gobbled another worm, the little robin had to agree. He was very relieved that he wasn't still lying in the cold, muddy gravel on the road! He finished one more worm and was satisfied. Sarah tucked the warm cloth around him and Mom carried his box to another room and set it where she could keep an eye on him during the night.

The house quieted down and the robin basked in the warmth of his box. What a predicament! Here he was, a few-days-old blind baby robin, and instead of being in his nest with his family, he was sitting in a cloth-lined box on a dresser being tended by strangers. In only a few hours, the course of his life had completely changed.

The darkness settled over him, making him sleepy. His eyelids drooped. For the first time in his life, he was going to fall asleep without his mother's warm breast blanketing him, without his father and the other birds singing goodnight songs, and without the trickling creek to lull him to sleep.

He stirred and snuggled deeper into his nest. He was warm, safe, and snug with a delicious meal in his tummy. What more could he want? From that moment on, all thoughts and memories of his parents and the nest in the tree began to fade.

Light

Light. It came slowly at first, almost unnoticeably. Every day seemed to be a little brighter than the last as the baby robin began to leave the blind darkness he had been born into. He was about a week old now and enjoying his new life with the Brown family, as he learned was their name. In the few short days since the terrible storm, he had almost forgotten that he was a robin and was beginning to feel like another member of their family.

Though blind during those first few days, the robin had learned a lot about his surroundings just through careful listening. He found that there were five in the Brown family: Dad, Mom, Sarah, and her two brothers. He knew that he was kept in a box in one of the sleeping rooms and fed with worms obtained from a place called the garden. On a couple of occasions, he was carted away in his box with the family and taken to unfamiliar places where strangers *oohed* and *ahhhed* over him.

Cheeper

    With each passing day, the visible world began to take shape before the little robin. He began to notice shadows moving when members of his family passed by, and then began to see the outlines of objects when he looked carefully. More detail appeared each day, until he was finally able to see everything around him clearly.

    The comfortable house where the Brown family lived was not too large and not too small. It had open, airy rooms and lots of sunlight streamed through the south windows. The baby robin liked it best when his box-nest was placed on a chest of drawers under the window where he could soak in the warm sunshine.

    With his eyes fully open, the robin could finally see what the Brown family looked like. True to his suspicion, these creatures had no wings to call their own and were forced to get around by way of their two legs. They were also much larger than he was. The hands that he had often felt cupped under his body were only a small part of the large bodies that loomed above him.

They hadn't any beaks, though their noses could possibly have been classified under a similar category. If they had any feathers, there was no way of knowing it, for they were always covered with clothing. The hair that grew from their heads could hardly be compared to the downy fluff of baby feathers that was beginning to grow on the little robin's body.

The members of his new family were quite different from average birds. Dad, tall and handsome with his thick, wavy hair, wasn't around much during the day; he left every morning to go to some place called "work." Mom was very pretty and spent most of her time tending to the needs of her family. She and Sarah were the ones who usually cared for him.

Sarah was a young teenager who looked so much like her mother that he could only tell them apart by their voices. Her brothers he had given up on—he couldn't tell them apart by either their appearances or their voices. The two of them were usually engaged in animated conversations about strange things called "iPods," "laptops," and "websites," but they sometimes took an interest in him and took a turn digging his worms and feeding him.

He would often sit and doze in his box, pondering the doings of his new family. They were different in many ways, yet there was one thing that the young robin did not find strange about the Brown family. Perhaps it was the only thing he had in common with them. That was their singing. Every morning and evening this family would gather in the living room to sing and pray.

The melodies always stirred something deep within his soul. He had heard the sweet strains of the hymns of praise before, but where? They spoke of a God of love who sent His Son to save the human race, whatever that meant. Yet it was as if the songs of praise were a part of what made him a robin—though it was his human family who sang them. It was a feeling that he could not fully understand or explain to himself, but he liked to pass the long hours of the day contemplating such things.

He often longed to join the family in singing the beautiful hymns, but didn't know how to even begin. Oh, he had a voice all right, and he liked to sit in his box and whisper and twitter softly to himself, or announce his hunger with a shrill *cheep*. His contented chirp of *cheep-er* had caused Mom and Sarah to name him Cheeper. But his chirping and tweeting were nothing in comparison with the songs his new family sang. Such songs of praise could only come from a heart that had been touched in a special way— a way he could not manufacture on his own. Maybe someday, though, he would learn the secret of singing such heart-felt songs.

It was an interesting world of perplexities and unanswered questions, but one thing was certain: Cheeper loved his new family with all his birdie heart, and he loved his new life. Certainly the future held only more happiness.

Growth

Cheeper stood and stretched, flapping his wings. He called loudly to see if Mom or Sarah was near. He wasn't really hungry, but rather just enjoyed the attention from his two nursemaids. No one came at first, so he called persistently louder and louder.

Finally, Sarah came, sighing, "All right Cheeper, are you *that* hungry?" She got the plastic container out of the fridge that held his worms, opened it, and selected a juicy specimen for him. He swallowed the worm and thanked her with a contented *cheep-er*.

Then came the part he had been waiting for. Sarah picked him up and held him in the palm of her hand and smoothed his feathers, crooning to him in the way that he loved so well.

"Mom," she called in the direction of the other room, "Cheeper's feathers are really filling in! He's starting to look like a real robin!" Cheeper relaxed under Sarah's gentle

32

touch, as she fanned out the feathers of his brown wings and admired his orange and white speckled breast. Downy baby feathers still clung to his throat—his only link to babyhood.

Cheeper had discarded the box-nest where he had spent his first week with the Brown family, now graduating to a smaller plastic container lined with a paper towel. This he only used for naps and bedtime, while during the day he would hop out onto the sunny top of the same old chest of drawers in the living room where he would observe his family's comings and goings.

He never ceased to take an interest in everything they did—from scurrying about getting ready for trips to town, clattering around in the cooking room preparing meals, or holding animated conversations on various topics.

To be sure, many of the Brown family's activities were quite strange. He had gotten used to their human customs by now, but he would never forget his initial surprise when he found out that the parents of this family, instead of poking food down their children's throats, let them fend for themselves at the meal table.

Even more surprising, there were never any worms or bugs on the menu—only indescribable dishes that they seemed to enjoy just as much as he enjoyed his worms. Not only that, but these humans would also have nothing to do with dirt of any kind and always ate clean food off sparkling clean dishware.

Young and uneducated though he was, even he knew that food tasted best fresh out of the ground where it was found crawling. Deep down, Cheeper felt sure that they were missing out on the nutrients and minerals that the dirt could give them, but he was part of the family now and would loyally defend them—no matter how strange!

Besides, just now there was something of even more interest and importance happening to Cheeper. He was beginning to feel… different. It was as if there was a surge of new strength flowing through his body and his wings. While just a week before he had been content to sit and think in his nest, now he was filled with an insatiable desire to *move*! He exercised his wings often during the day, standing on tiptoe and fluttering and flapping exuberantly.

The small chest of drawers where his plastic dish nest sat just didn't feel big enough anymore. Sometimes he would perch on the edge of his dresser-domain and peer over the edge to the floor, wondering if he would someday be able to get down there. Or he would gaze at the airy rooms adjoining the living room, wishing he could someday explore them. He wanted to *fly*! If only he had the courage to jump off the edge of the dresser, he would be able to soar effortlessly through the air!

So, one day he took the first plunge. He closed his eyes, strained every muscle upward, began flapping his wings violently, and *hopped*! Air rushed through his feathers, his feet left the dresser, and he had taken flight. He was flying! He was actually soaring! But his soaring hopes came crashing to the ground at the same time his body did. He sprawled on the carpeted living room floor and let out an embarrassed squawk.

Mom came running. "Cheeper, what happened?" He was too embarrassed to answer. Mom picked him up and straightened his ruffled feathers, but that didn't do much for his ruffled ego. His first flight had been a failure. He would never be able to fly again! Maybe he should just give up altogether. He crawled unhappily into his paper-towel-lined tub and allowed the waves of despair to overcome him.

He had been sure that he would be able to fly—yes, and a moment before he had been sure that he *was* flying. But it was no use! It had been a crash-landing instead. All those days of exercising his wings were wasted.

Yet, he could still feel the energy coursing through his wings from his attempted "flight." If nothing else, he had given his limbs more exercise. Besides, it had been rather exciting to feel the wind rushing through his feathers for the split second before he hit the ground. In fact, even the thought that he had been soaring effortlessly upward had been rather rewarding.

He had to admit that it was really just his hurt pride from his crash landing that was making him feel so bad. Perhaps if he forgot about that part and continued to exercise his wings every day, he would get stronger and stronger until he was able to fly without embarrassing himself.

No, Cheeper wasn't going to give up. He continued to stretch and flap his wings on top of his dresser, exercising and strengthening his muscles. It wasn't long before he again leapt from the dresser to see if he could fly. Only, this time, he waited until no one was around to see him make

36

any mistakes. He needn't have worried. He flapped and fluttered with all his might and succeeded in gliding down instead of falling, and he actually landed rather respectably on the carpeted living room floor, instead of in a disgraceful heap.

He couldn't have been happier, until he realized that he now had to get back *up* on his dresser. What to do now? No one was home, and although he tried his best to jump and flutter to the top, gravity always won and he found himself back on the floor. That is exactly where the Brown family found him when they got home from church.

"Cheeper's getting too big to be in the house." Dad shook his head. "We don't want to keep him caged up forever. He's got to start learning to be independent."

It did seem that every day Cheeper discovered how to do something that brought him more independence. One day Mom set his dish of dirt-covered worms on the top of the dresser so she could feed him. Hungry and anticipating his meal, Cheeper hopped onto the edge of the dish. He peered inside, gazing intently at the mass of black dirt in the dish. No worms were visible, but this was the place where Sarah or Mom always fished out his meals.

Wait! He cocked his head and listened. His ears picked up a faint sound. Yes, there it was again! It sounded like... well, it sounded like a worm! And right under Mom's grasping fingers, Cheeper excitedly jabbed his beak into the dirt directly where he had heard the sound and triumphantly emerged with a squirming worm, which soon disappeared down his throat.

Mom stood frozen with her hand still poised over the dish to pick out a worm—her mouth hanging open in amazement. She eagerly called Sarah, and they both watched as Cheeper repeated the experiment, again locating and pulling a worm from the dirt. After this, his dish of worms was always left on the top of his dresser for him to select and eat one whenever he felt hungry.

Then came the monumental day when the world as Cheeper knew it suddenly became a lot bigger! It was a sunny summer afternoon like any other when Sarah took him in her cupped hands and carried him outside for the first time. Cheeper squinted and blinked his eyes in the bright sunshine. So this is where the sunbeams came from that danced on his dresser and warmed his back through the window!

And he had once thought the blue house to be an airy, open expanse! Compared to this wonderful place that Sarah called "outside," the house seemed small and confining. Lush, green foliage stretched in every direction, unhindered by walls of any kind. Overhead, there was no ceiling, except for a beautiful, blue canopy miles above dotted with trailing white clouds.

Although he still sat in the confinement of Sarah's cupped hands, Cheeper suddenly felt light and free with the wide expanse all around him—an exciting and exhilarating feeling of freedom that he had never experienced while inside the little house.

Soon Sarah set him down on the hard-packed dirt amidst all kinds of different plants and vegetables. She took what looked like a very large spoon with a wooden handle and shoved it into the ground. "Come on, Cheeper," she called. He answered with his typical *cheep-er* and hopped curiously over to her. He cocked his head and watched her turn over the shovel, exposing the soft, black dirt underneath. What was she doing? Why was she turning the dirt over? He soon found out.

"There's one!" Sarah suddenly pointed to the mound of dirt she had just overturned. And sure enough! There, wiggling temptingly in the soil, lay a cool, slim earthworm. Cheeper excitedly snatched the worm up and gobbled it down.

Now he had caught on to the idea and waited expectantly for what the next shovel-full would dig up. He was quickly rewarded, this time with a fat, white grub. Just about every shovel-full of dirt exposed some kind of worm

Cheeper

or bug, and Cheeper ate until he was stuffed! Then, after saying a satisfied *cheep-er*, he nestled down under the leaves of some broad-leafed plants and took a nap while Sarah finished cultivating.

That evening Cheeper overheard Sarah telling the family about his first experience outdoors. "He seemed to like it!" Her words woke Cheeper from near sleep. "And letting him eat his worms right out of the garden is much easier than digging the worms myself and feeding them to him later. He gets fed, and I get the garden weeded at the same time."

"So, you're killing two birds with one stone?" Sarah's brother's voice held a note of teasing. "Actually, more like killing two worms with one shovel!" Everyone chuckled.

40

"Killing two birds with one stone," whatever that meant, didn't sound very pleasant, but eating his worms right out of the garden certainly was! It was so nice to be out in the sunshine and fresh air, and the food tasted so much better when it came fresh from the ground instead of from a plastic dish.

From then on, either Sarah or Mom would take Cheeper outside with them at his feeding time to let him pick his worms right out of the dirt himself—and he couldn't have been happier with the new arrangement.

He loved being outdoors. There was something soothing and peaceful about the soft summer breezes, the puffy clouds floating by high overhead, cottonwood fluff drifting lazily on the breeze, the sunshine and shadows, the lush green grass and foliage, and the happy songs of birds filling the air. It was hard to explain, but somehow the serenity of summertime matched how he felt inside. His life was simple, his needs were met, and not a cloud blocked the warmth of the sunshine in his life.

Cheeper still practiced flying and improved with every attempt, but he still could only glide down to the ground. If only he could start from higher up, he probably would be able to do a little better. The dresser in the house was the highest up he had been, though. That is, until one day not long after, when Sarah took him on a mysterious trip outdoors—and it wasn't even his mealtime!

Before he could figure out what was going on, she had tossed him high into the air and let him flutter to the ground. He enjoyed the feeling of flying high above the ground and said a happy *cheep-er*. Again and again Sarah threw him upwards and let him flutter back to the ground. It became a daily routine, and little by little Cheeper found himself being able to stay in the air longer and fly higher and farther.

One evening, as Sarah hurled Cheeper upwards, he flapped and fluttered so hard that he was able to turn himself in a different direction. Spying an overhanging limb by the garden just ahead, Cheeper bent every effort on staying in flight until he could grasp the very bottom branch.

For the first time ever, his flight did not bring him back to the ground. Sarah hurried over only to find him far out of her reach. Cheeper was elated, despite Sarah's obvious dismay.

"Cheeper, come! Cheeper, Cheeper! Come on boy!" Sarah pleaded with him, holding out a finger for him to fly down to.

Each time she called, he answered her with a polite *cheep-er*, but there was no way he was going to give up the opportunity of his unexpected new-found freedom. The sun began to set and the blue sky turned to a dusky gray.

Sarah's calls for her pet grew distressed. Finally her hand dropped to side and her last call of "Cheeper!" sounded exasperated. She turned and hurried towards the house. Cheeper twittered delightedly! What an exciting turn of events!

Sarah soon returned, with the rest of the family in tow. "Look, Dad, he's up there just out of reach, and I don't know what to do! We can't leave him out here all night!"

Dad wasn't tall enough to reach the branch either, and Cheeper obeyed none of the families' entreaties to come down for the night. He always answered them with his usual *cheep-er*, but he wouldn't budge.

Sarah's brother found a stick that was long enough to reach the robin and lifted it close to him. They were probably hoping he would hop onto it to be lowered down, but he only climbed higher out of reach and said a firm *cheep-er* to tell the family that he was right where he wanted to be and determined to stay there.

"Well, there's nothing else we can do!" Dad finally gave up and turned to head for the house, Sarah's brothers following. With one last plea for cooperation, which went unheeded, Sarah and Mom turned away too.

Cheeper

"I hope Cheeper will be okay through the night!" Sarah threw one last worried glance over her shoulder at her robin.

Mom's voice drifted faintly back to Cheeper on the still night air as she and Sarah disappeared around the corner of the house. "Don't worry, Sarah, you'll get him to come to you in the morning...."

It was too bad that he had caused his family so much distress, but they were overly alarmed. He was a big boy now—quite able to fend for himself for one night! He wasn't the least bit frightened. The friendly coolness of the night closed in around him as the last rays of sunshine disappeared from the western horizon.

High overhead in the large arching sky, little pinpricks of light began to appear and twinkle down on him, and golden beams of soft light eradiating from a paler, sleepier sort of sun created peaceful shadows on the garden.

Soft, questioning hoots from a nearby tree were answered from a tree on the other side of house in the same questioning manner. A slight breeze rustled the leaves of the trees, and birdies murmured their last goodnights to one another.

As the stillness of night descended, the sound of trickling water caught Cheeper's attention. It was a soothing sound, unexplainably alluring. He had to get closer. Spotting the branch of another tree not far away, he fluttered to it, and then on to another tree limb, and then another. In this way—flying from tree to tree—he eventually found himself sitting in a tree high above the outline of a rough, dirt road and a dancing, gurgling stream of water.

Something about the sound was very familiar. It was as if he had been there before. But it couldn't be, so he dismissed the thought, tucked his head underneath a wing, and let the gurgling song of the creek lull him to sleep.

<u>Change</u>

"Cheeperrrr…. Cheeeeeeperrrrr…."

Cheeper opened his eyes and blinked slowly. Where in creation was he? He took a deep breath of cold, fresh air and shook his head to clear the foggy dream that still blocked his vision.

Tree branches and leaves slowly came into focus, sparkling as low rays of sunlight hit the droplets of water covering them. He shivered. Apparently, the droplets of water covered him as well. He shook his feathers out and fluffed them up over his body. There, now he was awake!

"Cheeeeeeeperrrrrrrr…."

The call startled Cheeper. He recognized that voice—it was Sarah. Peering through the leaves, Cheeper saw Sarah and Mom at the upper end of the garden, each clothed in a fuzzy robe, their disheveled hair framing their worried faces. In an instant, the recollection of the night before flooded back, and Cheeper quickly gave an

46

answering call to his family.

"I heard him, Mom, I heard him!" Sarah grabbed her mom's arm and pulled her in the direction of the call.

Moving across the branch until he was out in the open, Cheeper continued to answer Mom and Sarah's calls until they finally spotted him. He was glad to see them and fluttered willingly down to Sarah's outstretched hand. Soon he was cuddled in her hands. After that, he noticed that she was careful to not toss him into the air near any trees.

Still, the whole family seemed to realize that he was ready for more freedom. They were always careful to bring him in at night, but he was now allowed to spend most of the day outside in the little oak tree close by the house, or, if they were working in the garden, in one of the stubby little apple trees nearby. From those vantage points, he could observe all the outdoor activities.

The little woods surrounding the blue house on the hill were always alive with a bustle of birds. All day long, they filled the air with their songs. Cheeper heard them calling to one another as they passed by high above, and sometimes a squabbling pair dashed past the tree where he sat. None of them paid much attention to him. They all seemed to have their own circle of friends and never even noticed the lone, little robin sitting by himself.

One day, that changed. He was sitting all by himself in the crook of the apple tree, watching Mom pull weeds in the garden when he heard a fluttering sound. He turned his head and saw the most beautiful robin sitting on a branch not far away. She was obviously young, like himself, with her lovely speckled breast and light brown feathers, and for a moment he could only sit and gaze at her in captivated silence.

Then the lady robin hopped over and introduced herself. He immediately felt at ease in her presence, as if he had always known her. For a long while, they just chattered and twittered and got acquainted, and then Lady Robin coaxed him to follow her from the apple tree to see some of her favorite spots. The sweet, musical tone of her voice was impossible to resist, and so he fluttered after her. He didn't

48

know it yet, but he had found his mate. It was love at first sight.

Cheeper never again came to the Browns when they called him. At first, he tried to give an answering *cheep-er* to their calls, just to let them know that he was safe and well, but eventually he forgot to respond at all. He was no longer a member of their family. He had found something better— he had found out that he was a robin!

Now the dawn of each new day brought with it an exciting thrill of potential. There was so much he had to learn, so much that his new lady friend could teach him. He often shook his head as he remembered how much he used to think he knew. Compared to Lady, he knew nothing.

It was she who showed him where and when to find the fattest worms. She was the one who taught him how to catch bugs right out of the air, how to fluff up his feathers to keep warm and dry when it rained, and what dangers he needed to avoid—poisonous berries, cats, and especially hawks.

Cheeper didn't know why she made such a big deal out of these "dangers." Why, he had occasionally seen the Brown family's two outdoor cats roaming around, but they had never bothered or even noticed him. She hadn't even mentioned the only danger he knew of—storms, with their flashing lightning and booming thunder that always filled

Cheeper

him with unexplainable terror.

One day, when he was again complaining at Lady's over-cautiousness, she turned her clear eyes toward him and told him, as he listened in shocked silence, how a hawk had gotten her father. Her mother had not lived long after that. She had been just old enough to care for herself.

So she was alone in the world—but not so anymore! Now they had each other. Cheeper spent every possible moment with Lady Robin. They did everything together... except singing. Cheeper loved to listen to Lady sing. She had a voice that was so sweet and precious that it never failed to melt his heart.

He longed to add his voice to hers. Sometimes he would try to, but his attempts proved that he didn't know what notes to sing and his tunes always lacked

50

something—a certain earnest emotion that pervaded all her melodies. How was it that this robin, who had gone through the tragedy and heartache of losing her parents, could still sing such heartfelt songs of praise to the Creator, while he, whose life had been easy and happy, could not?

It was not as if he didn't know the songs Lady sang. In fact, he was sure that he had heard them before somewhere. They vaguely reminded him of the beautiful songs that his human family had sung every morning and evening. Interestingly, the Brown family's songs praised a God of love, while Lady's songs were in praise of the Creator.

Could the God of love *be* the Creator? Cheeper hadn't thought much about the Creator. Of course, the Creator was the One who made everything and the One who was praised in the songs of most every bird. Yet, a *loving* Creator—a personal *friend*? That was an entirely new thought. If the Creator *was* a loving God, could it be that He cared not only for humans, but also for robins and other birds... and for him?

Cheeper shook his head. It couldn't be true. What was most important was that he now had a friend to love, and he was sure that nothing would ever separate him from Lady!

Part II
Autumn

Flight

Cheeper sighed wearily and settled down onto the branch of the maple tree between the blue house and the garden. His wings and legs ached from overuse! He and Lady had been searching for food all day. The weather was turning decidedly cold, and an extra layer of fat was needed to block out the chilly wind that often swept across the little valley.

It didn't help that food was getting increasingly harder to find. It was as if the worms were burrowing deeper and deeper into the warm earth. He and Lady were hardly ever able to find one on the cold surface anymore. A recent frost had killed a good part of the bug supply, and nearby berry bushes had almost been picked clean.

Thankfully, Lady had chanced upon a large mass of hibernating bugs in a crevice under a fallen log that they both had feasted on. The log was a long way from home, though, and Cheeper was glad to finally give his wings a rest.

Lady settled on the branch beside him and twittered a tune softly to herself. Lady.... Cheeper shook his head in wonder. Always a song on her beak, no matter how tired she was. Cheeper ruffled his feathers into a warmer heap on his back and slowly drank in his surroundings.

High in the treetops bordering the creek, huge flocks of blackbirds congregated, filling the air with their loud calls. In the garden not far away, he saw two figures of his former family working away. They were pulling up vines and vegetation and filling boxes and buckets with brightly colored vegetables. Gone were the neat rows of lush, green plants, leaving the ground looking brown and bare.

In fact, everything was beginning to look brown and bare. It was only a few short weeks ago that the leaves had turned color. Those had been exhilarating weeks in which Cheeper's world had gone from pretty to beautiful. Not even Lady had known that leaves could be any other color than green.

And now the vibrant golden-browns, reds, and yellows were fading into dull browns. The grass was withering, and the perky little flowers that lined the side of the house had all shriveled up. Cheeper sighed again. Death and decay seemed to be on every side, and it made his heart

54

ache to look at it. Would the grass and leaves ever come back?

Conditions only seemed to get worse. Low, gray clouds skirted the sky for days on end, blown in by the heavy, cold winds. The dead, faded leaves were torn from the trees and flung to the ground, leaving the thin, naked branches exposed. Cheeper couldn't understand what had happened to his beautiful, happy world. Would the sunshine always be blocked by the clouds?

Not even the depressing weather seemed to dampen Lady's spirits. She patiently searched far and wide for food with Cheeper, and when they found something edible, her songs of thanksgiving were soothing to his discontented spirit.

It was hard to be thankful when he had to search hours just to find a few bugs or berries. And he could have bet his last worm that there weren't as many hours in the day to do the searching anymore–except that he couldn't remember when he had *had* his last worm!

Frost fell almost every night now, and Cheeper had to snuggle next to Lady in order to keep warm, his feathers fluffed up over his bare legs and his head tucked beneath his wing. It was always hard to leave the cozy branch and venture out into the frosty morning air, but it also felt good

to get the blood pumping through his wings after the long, cold nights.

One morning, Cheeper awoke to find a light dusting of snow covering everything, including him and Lady. With twitters of surprise and excitement, he and Lady shook the tingling flakes from their feathers and bounded from their warm branch to survey the white world around them.

Even though a chilling wind blew, warm blood surged through their bodies as they played and chased each other through the glistening, snowy woods, dodging snowflakes as they went. It was the first time that either of them had ever seen snow. It reminded Cheeper of the cottonwood fluff that had drifted from the trees in the summer, but it was definitely much, much colder!

As beautiful and exciting as the snow was, it quickly covered any remaining sources of food. The time had come to move on in search of warmer weather and a better food supply.

Later that day, while Lady scratched in the snow, trying to find some dried berries that might have fallen from a bush, Cheeper left her for a moment and flew to his favorite haunt, the tree above the road and creek. He glanced around at the barren trees and at the creek, its trickling waters slowly being silenced by icy fingers. Then his eyes fell on the blue house on the hill.

The Brown family…. He had nearly forgotten about them. During the past month, he had caught a glimpse every now and then of certain family members going for walks, taking care of their pets, raking leaves, and harvesting the garden vegetables. As he gazed at the house, faint memories of Sarah's warm hands cupped under him, the cozy plastic-dish-nest, and their family-time singing stirred in his mind. Did they still remember him? Did they ever think about him? Would he ever see them again?

For a moment, he just sat there, lost in thought, until he heard Lady cheeping for him to come. The great moment had arrived. Cheeper glanced at Lady and his excitement was mirrored in her eyes. Simultaneously, they spread their wings and took flight, soaring higher and higher and swiftly leaving the land of cold and snow behind them. What kind of adventures awaited them in the days ahead?

Adventure

The air was filled with twitters and chirps as birds of all shapes and sizes called excitedly to each other from the branches of a leafless berry bush where they finally filled their stomachs to the full. Cheeper and Lady had flown for many hours before they finally spotted the thicket of berry bushes. They weren't hard to find, either—Cheeper and Lady had heard the din of noise rising from the clearing long before they even saw the bushes. Finally, they could rest their wings and eat the dried berries that still clung to the icy branches.

While Lady chattered happily to the birds around her, Cheeper ate his berries in shy silence. He enjoyed conversing with Lady, but there was something about this throng of vocal birds that made him feel rather tongue-tied.

The berries soon disappeared. Gradually, the other birds moved off in groups, until just the robins were left. With a satisfying meal filling their tummies, many robins

Cheeper

took naps. Cheeper didn't realize how exhausted he really was until he closed his eyes and leaned against Lady, who was also tucking her head under her wing for some rest. The tiring search for food in the preceding weeks had left little time for sleep.

Pinpricks of ice on his face awakened Cheeper. A chilling wind was swirling tiny snowflakes through the air. Lady, too, was slowly blinking awake and stretching her wings. His stomach growled. A few of the robins were hopping among the crisp, crunching leaves beneath the bushes, scratching about to see if any dried berries had fallen there. They didn't seem to be having much luck, so there was no point in joining them. Cheeper huddled closer to Lady and fluffed his feathers into a thicker mass about his body.

The robins gave up their search for berries and joined the flock in the bush. Questioning glances were exchanged from robin to robin. What now? One outgoing robin finally took initiative, spread his wings, and rose slowly from the bush. The rest of the robins took flight after him. With a bound off the branch Lady joined them, but Cheeper trailed after her rather reluctantly. Of course, there was safety in numbers, but it would have been much more pleasant if he and his sweet Lady could have journeyed on alone together.

Still, it was exciting! He had now traveled well outside of his normal flying range. His adventure had begun! He had been keeping his eyes peeled for the dangers of the outside world that Lady had warned him of—cats, eagles, and, above all, hawks—but so far he had not seen any signs of peril. In fact, the landscape still was very similar to the one that he had left behind.

Day after day, Cheeper and Lady wove their way slowly southward with the flock, staying just ahead of the cold winds and snowstorms and moving from one source of food to another. No two days were alike. At first, each new day thrilled Cheeper with excitement, but his adventuresome spirit began to wear thin as the weather grew colder and it became more difficult to find a lasting supply of food.

Cheeper

Anything edible that could be found was welcomed. Once, hunger had driven them to try some of the scraps of... something... Cheeper liked to think it was some kind of old fruit. Maybe it was best that he hadn't known exactly what it was that he was eating, and at least it helped to calm the hunger pains in his stomach. After a few nights where the temperatures dropped really low and freezing winds blew, though, the "fruit" was too frozen to eat.

They were up the next morning at the first gray light of dawn to begin again their frantic search for another food supply. Each member of the group was to be on lookout for two things: dangers and food. Even Lady found little time for singing, but her cheerful spirit remained as undaunted as ever. The chilling winds blew them onward, and they didn't stop until the blackness of night made it dangerous to continue. The group of robins huddled together to stay warm and listened to each other's stomachs growl. It was a long night.

Glad cries, mixed with sighs of relief, arose from the whole group the next morning when they stumbled upon a rotting, tumbledown barn. Cheeper fluttered in single file with the other robins through the crooked frame of an upper window. They settled themselves along one of the thick, wide rafter beams.

It was dark and dusty in the barn. Dim light from outside filtered through cracks in the walls, glinting off of millions of particles of dust stirred up by the wind. The whole building creaked as the wind rushed around it in howling fury. But at least this structure offered them protection from the icy gale outside!

Cheeper's eyes were finally adjusting to the darkness. The floor of the building below was cluttered with piles of strange objects. Cheeper cocked his head and squinted at the items. They looked solid and cold, and were all different shapes and sizes. At one time in their distant past they may have been bright and shiny, but they were now tarnished with rust and dirt.

Cheeper sniffed the air. The building smelled musty, with a faint, sweet, grassy smell. Perhaps that had something to do with the soggy bales of dried grasses stacked in the far corner. Cobwebs hung from the ceilings and rafters, swaying slightly in the breeze that found its way through the cracks in the walls.

The robins were making themselves at home. Lady and some of the others were settling down and fluffing their feathers over their legs for a rest. The others hopped from rafter to rafter and joined Cheeper in examining their surroundings.

Cheeper

Cheeper shifted his gaze to the twisted ceiling overhead. He hopped over to the narrow joists where the ceiling met the walls. Was that a slight movement? Cheeper stopped and stared intently at a crack between two boards. A loud cheap of excitement escaped his beak, bringing all the robins to their feet in hurry. They rushed to where he was excitedly grabbing at something down between two of the joist boards. He had discovered a cluster of dormant bugs sleeping in the crack!

The robins pressed close around him, straining their necks to reach over shoulders and grab one of the delicious, juicy bugs. There just wasn't enough room for all of them to get their fill. More exploration revealed many cracks and crevices in the building that were filled with hibernating bugs and beetles.

They feasted and rested in that barn for many days, until the bug supply was exhausted. One by one, the robins followed each other through the little, twisted window and winged their way southward again. Thankfully, the merciless blast of chilling wind had stilled to only an icy breeze.

Still, it was hard to leave. Cheeper looked back over his shoulder as the group left the barn further and further behind. Despite its ramshackle outward appearance, that building had character and appeal in its own way. Cheeper had grown to love it during his short stay.

The group no longer called excitedly to each other as they flew, but all focused on reaching the next safe haven as quickly as possible. Far below, the brown, barren landscape inched by. It seemed to move along so slowly, and yet turned into the miles that had carried him far from home so quickly. Time was a little like that. The hours dragged on endlessly when they were in search of food, and yet Cheeper couldn't even remember how many weeks had passed since he first began his adventure. He couldn't even keep track of how many new places he'd stayed or how many new foods he'd eaten.

One day, a drizzling rain descended on the silent flock of flapping robins. The cold, hard droplets soaked chillingly through Cheeper's feathers. The other robins were calling to each other. Did anyone spot a place where they could find protection from the rain? Cheeper let his sharp eyes rove over the landscape. A green, leaf-covered tree would have been a welcome site, but all the barren trees below were just as exposed to the rain as the robins and wouldn't offer much protection.

The wind picked up. The droplets of rain weren't just wet; they were beginning to feel icy too. They stung Cheeper's eyes. He bent his head to the onslaught and flapped his wings all the harder. Lady and the other birds were picking up speed as well.

Cheeper stole a glance at Lady. She looked positively weary. They were all weary! They would have to find shelter soon, but where? Blinding white snow began to swirl in with the mix of icy rain. It was hard to see the lead robin who was flying only a few robins ahead of Cheeper. There was no denying it: They had been caught in an early blizzard!

Soon everything had become a white, howling blur. The wind seemed bent on tearing the flock of robins apart until they were separated from each other in the blinding snow and darkness. Cheeper felt the tiny hand of fear begin to clutch at his heart. He had to stay close to Lady as the fierce wind swept them where it wished. He had to keep the gray shadows of the other birds in sight through the thickly flying snow.

He strained every muscle in his wings and pressed closer to the flock. How much longer could they go on like this? Their last meal had been so long ago; it was no longer fueling them on or heating their bodies. Cheeper could feel the cold wind and icy snow chilling his limbs. The fear grew. It was now tightly grasping his pounding heart.

Cheeper looked at Lady by his side, her head bent to the wind and wings flapping vigorously. She look calm, not frightened. Everything about her was peaceful, though earnest in her effort to combat the elements.

Then, out of the whirling whiteness emerged the dark shape of something large and square not far ahead. It was some sort of large building, which disappeared into the whiteness above and below. The flock flew along the side of the building and rounded the corner. The large solid wall now blocked the wind, but the swirling snow still made it hard to see. A large indent appeared in the side of the wall, and the Cheeper and the other robins fluttered eagerly to rest on the wide ledge. Here they were sheltered from the wind and snow.

For a moment, Cheeper just stood there looking over the group of bedraggled robins, their chests heaving and their feathers wet and ruffled, and suddenly his legs gave out beneath him. He sank down wearily onto his breast beside Lady, his whole body trembling. They were safe! They weren't going to die! But they could have.

Cheeper shook the chilling thought from his mind. What he needed now was rest—and lots of it! He closed his eyes and willed his muscles to relax. His pounding heart began to slow back to normal. He had yet to experience the dangers of hawks, cats, or poisonous berries, but he now knew the danger of a winter storm.

Fright

The wind continued to shriek and howl and drive the blinding snow past in a thick whirlwind, but on top of the wide ledge the robins were sheltered by the jutting walls of the building. Cheeper's head nodded and the sounds of the storm lulled him to sleep.

In his dreams, a shrieking, white bird flew round and round him until he was dizzy and his ears rang. Finally the white bird left, growing smaller and smaller on the horizon, its shrieks getting fainter and fainter. Yet all was not quiet. From the other direction approached a huge flock of migrating geese. Soon hundreds of honking geese were whooshing past him. The noise was deafening!

Cheeper awoke with a start. The air was clean and still. Buildings of every shape and size surrounded them as far as he could see, which wasn't very far considering the tall obstructions that blocked the clear, blue sky from view.

A layer of snow blanketed the robins and the ledge. The air was chilly, but the storm had indeed subsided. But the honking, whooshing noise of the geese persisted. Or was it geese? It didn't sound quite the same as the honking he and Lady had heard while they were still back home. And this honking was not as loud as the geese in his dream—a little farther away perhaps.

Quietly, so as to not awaken Lady, Cheeper shook the snow from his body and kicked it away from his legs and shuffled to the edge of the ledge. The loud sound of those strange, whooshing geese rose from below him. Cheeper peered cautiously over the edge. Not far below a myriad of large, shiny objects of various colors and shapes whooshed past, honking and making quite a racket.

Well, they certainly weren't anything like the long-necked geese that flew south in V-shaped troops! Cheeper had never seen anything like them! Then again, maybe he had! These were the same vehicles that inched along winding paths far below them as the group of robins flew high in the sky. What's more, he had often seen one or two such vehicles sitting next to the little blue house or passing by on the dusty gravel road. But to see so many in such a noisy crowd was definitely a new experience!

Slushy snow sloshed around the vehicles and the morning sunshine glinted off the shiny sides. The sunshine

Cheeper

was warm on Cheeper's cheeks and not a cloud could be seen in the sky—or, what little sky he could see beyond the tall buildings.

Lady and the other robins were finally shaking the snow from their wings and joining Cheeper on the edge of the ledge. Lady hopped next to him and gazed out over scene around them. Little droplets of water dripped from the edges of the rooftops in the warmth of the sun. Far below, tiny people bustled up and down the edges of the buildings, getting in and out of vehicles, and entering and exiting the buildings.

Always the never-ending lines of noisy vehicles flew by. Hundreds had passed by already and still the lines continued, all of them going somewhere and seemingly in a great hurry. What could be so urgent? Perhaps they too were on a quest for warmth, food, and shelter.

Speaking of food, was there any food to be found in this bustling city? Even though the sun was melting the early snow and raising the temperatures, it was still too cold for any worms to be found.

Even if there were worms in the ground below, the robins would have had a hard time getting them out—there were no bare patches of ground in sight. Every inch of ground was covered with solid buildings and walls, walking paths of smooth gray rock, and paths for the vehicles of some hard, dark-colored coating painted with bright lines. There wasn't a berry bush in sight anywhere, nor a fallen, bug-filled log. Just where were they going to find food?

Cheeper shifted restlessly. He was hungry. They had put in a long time and a lot of flying since their last meal. There wasn't any food in sight, and they weren't going to find any just sitting there. As if in agreement, the other robins stretched their wings and readied themselves for flight.

They set off with what little energy they had left. As they flapped upwards and the obstructing buildings grew smaller beneath them, the view opening before them took Cheeper's breath away. The buildings and hard roads filled with noisy vehicles and bustling people spread out as far as he could see. Where would they find food here? Still, they had to try. Surely there would be a fruit tree or a hollow log somewhere. The sun crawled upwards and was making short work of the early snow, and still neither Cheeper nor his companions could spot any signs of food below. The sun was high overhead before they finally spotted something that looked promising.

They circled and lowered down until they landed on the edge of a huge bin filled with garbage. Cheeper surveyed the contents with interest. Here was a place he had never been for a meal before, one to add to his growing list of new and strange experiences.

He followed the other birds' lead and hopped from the edge into the bin, landing on a bulging, bouncy, black bag. The bin was filled with these tied up bags, along with numerous large metal objects, but there were also loose scraps of food. Mostly moldy, stale bread, but there were some pieces of half-eaten fruit to be found in the rubble.

Cheeper was so hungry he could have eaten the metal objects, except that they were a little too big to fit down his throat. The bread upset his stomach slightly, but at least it satisfied him.

Finally, the robins had their fill. They took flight once again. The endless buildings and vehicles crept past below and stretched out in every direction. Cheeper sighed and looked upwards into the big blue expanse of sky. If he never saw another building again or heard another car honk he wouldn't regret it. At least the warm sunshine had nearly melted all the snow. There were only a few clumps here and there in dark, shaded corners.

The group of robins spent the night crowded into a little shelter at the top of a towering spire on a grand-looking building with lots of arched windows that glinted in different colors in the setting sun. The little shelter at the top of the spire would have been the perfect home for birds, except for the fact that it instead housed a large, cold metal object in the shape of an upside-down tulip. Cheeper and the other robins had to squeeze in around it.

The next day Cheeper awoke bright and early and hurried to nudge Lady awake and to call the others out of their slumbers. It was time they were on their way. This time Cheeper took the lead of the flock. All the others were still blinking sleep from their eyes.

As they flew on and on, hour after hour, the tall buildings became sparser, replaced instead with tightly packed rows of houses. The streets were comparatively quieter here. At least there were signs of vegetation around the houses—leafless trees and decorative shrubs dotting tiny lawns where grass had certainly been growing a few months ago.

Cheeper

For breakfast, the robins feasted on mushy fruit that littered the ground under an abandoned fruit tree behind one of the houses. The fruit was well past its prime, but at least it satisfied their stomachs. Cheeper pecked hungrily at yet another piece of fruit he was sharing with Lady. It was too bad the humans hadn't known about this yummy food supply so close at hand. They were rushing here and there almost as frantically as the robins, when they had a tree full of fruit going to waste right in their back yard. Oh well—in this case, the humans' loss was the robins' gain.

He had to admit that this might not be a bad place to spend the winter. The scores of buildings would provide countless havens of refuge from the snowstorms, and the humans would always be close at hand to supply the large bins with discarded food for the robins to feast on. But the crowded city was lacking something—a peace and solitude that could be found only in quiet meadows and shady forests.

Cheeper took one last peck at the piece of fruit. He was stuffed. It felt so good to finally have a full stomach! Cheeper and Lady joined the other robins who were settling on the top of a nearby white picket fence to rest their heavy bellies. Cheeper sat still for only a moment. He stood first on one foot, then the other. He scuttled impatiently back and forth across the fence board. After what seemed like forever, the other birds finally spread their wings and followed Cheeper into the air, though some did so rather reluctantly. Excitement gripped Cheeper's heart. He couldn't wait to see something other than buildings and paved ground. Oh, would the lines of buildings and roads never end?

The sun was high overhead before the last building finally disappeared and the beautiful open landscape spread before them. Sure, the leaves were gone and food was scarce, but the quiet countryside, tree-filled forests, and grassy fields were a whole lot better than the noisy, bustling city built of hard rock and pavement. Out here there was peace.

After that, although they passed over many bustling cities and crowded towns, Cheeper always voted for finding a more remote place to take shelter and food.

One day, as they flew over a quiet country park, a member of the group noticed a small family throwing pieces of bread to a little flock of ducks. Here was an opportunity to fill their stomachs with something more than old fruit. Circling high above and then softly descending into the bushes a short distance away, the group of robins politely waited for the ducks to finish.

The young, laughing boy and his little, giggling sister soon exhausted their resources of bread cubes and their mother hustled them away. The ducks waddled back to the pond, and finally their turn came. Thanks to the sloppy ducks, many bread crumbs were left on the ground. Cheeper, Lady, and the other robins hungrily devoured the leftovers.

Most of the robins never sat still for a moment. As quickly as they pecked at a crumb, they jerked their heads up and surveyed their surroundings for any signs of danger. Cheeper, however, did not see any cause for alarm in this peaceful park.

A few young children played gleefully on a contraption that swung them back and forth much like he had often done on a wind-tossed tree branch, and a group of young boys were digging in a large box of sand— probably looking for worms. Certainly they would be of no harm to a flock of robins. Cheeper calmly kept his eyes on his meal. Humans were nothing to be afraid of; they could be trusted.

A moment later, something hard and cold grazed past Cheeper's head and landed in the middle of the pecking group. For a split second, each feathered body froze in place. In the next instant, they surged to life, raising a commotion of squawking and fluttering as they rose from the ground to take cover.

Behind them a shower of rocks and sticks aimed at their departing bodies rained down from the group of seemingly harmless little boys, who now shouted and yelled in great delight over their "ambush."

From the safety of nearby bushes, the robins paused to catch their breath. Cheeper's little heart pounded so swiftly in his chest that it hurt. Perhaps he needed to be on better guard after all—even when all looked safe and harmless. It wouldn't do for him to rely on the others around him to keep on the lookout for danger for him. The group fluttered into the air once again to continue on their way. Hawks, cats, and poisonous berries, Lady had told him. Well, she forgot to mention early winter storms and innocent-looking little boys.

It was hard to stay on guard all the time, though. The beautiful scenery passing below as the robins glided along captivated Cheeper, until with a start he tore his eyes away to glance furtively about for dangers. He had been distracted yet again!

Mornings were especially hard. The sun rose with beams of golden splendor. The clouds of mist slowly ascended from marshes in breathtaking beauty. The group of robins had been up since the crack of dawn, scouting about for something to fill their stomachs. As usual, Lady flew close by Cheeper's side, the steady rhythm of her beating wings matching his. He knew that she too was enjoying the beauty of a new morning.

Perhaps they were all enraptured with the sunrise, or perhaps the direction of the wind was such that they did not sense the danger that slowly descended upon them— not until a bloodcurdling cry sounded directly behind the group. Cheeper's heart stopped momentarily and his body went cold and numb with fright. Confusion immediately broke out in their ranks, as the robins squawked and screeched and rushed frantically away from the hungry hawk bearing down on them.

Before the group could scatter, though, Lady's voice rang out, calling to everyone to stay together! She swept past Cheeper and, with a flick of her tail, turned her course downward, leading the group on a descending path toward a thicket a trees below. *Follow me; stay together*, her calls commanded, and all the robins immediately obeyed. Pressing as closely together as possible, the group surged onward with the hawk nearly on their tails.

They zipped and zoomed their way into the dense grove of trees, flying as fast as their wings could carry them, dodging trees and skimming through small openings in the

dense overgrowth, all the while following Lady's lead. Yet the persistent hawk still pursued them. At least his size was to their advantage. He, being larger, was greatly impeded by their wild course through the thick underbrush.

Quick as flash, Lady darted to the left, making her way toward a large fallen tree. Following her change of course, Cheeper and the other robins could make out a small opening in the side of this log. One by one, the robins squeezed into the safety of the hollow log, the last robin entering with a frightened *cheep!* just as the hawk's sharp talons grasped unsuccessfully for his tail feathers. They had reached safety just in time! They huddled together, hearts pounding, listening to the hawk scream angrily at them from outside the log.

Cheeper

The hawk, muttering to himself, paced up and down the length of the log for a while. If he was hoping that the robins were going to eventually emerge right under his nose, he would be sorely disappointed. A good hour passed before he gave up hope and flew away in search of something else to eat.

Still, for several hours afterward, the robins remained in the safety of the hollow log. Cheeper's racing heart slowly calmed, but his thoughts tumbled on. What a marvel Lady was! She had saved their lives. She had kept her cool and thought of the others when they had all panicked and thought only of themselves. When they were about to scatter, she directed them to stick together. This enabled them to give support to each other and prevented the hawk from picking out and pursuing only the weaker ones.

How did she know what to do? Cheeper finally turned to her and twittered his question. She took a deep breath before answering. She had told him long ago that she had lost her parents as a young robin, barely old enough to survive on her own. But she had never told him exactly how she lost them. A hawk had attacked. Her father had separated from her and her mother in hopes that the hawk would pursue him instead of them. They had never seen him again. Her mother had died of a broken heart.

80

Cheeper shuddered. How could Lady be so peaceful and happy when such a terrible tragedy had happened in her life?

Part III
Winter

<u>*Sorrow*</u>

Cheeper floated lazily on the south wind, enjoying the feel of the warm sunshine on his back. He and Lady had finally reached the end of the trail. No more violent snowstorms on their tails. No more did they have to live in uncertainty, not knowing when or where they would find their next meal. The new landscape provided the two robins with warmer weather, along with plenty of fresh worms and bugs, and everything two birds could want to spend the winter season.

They and a few other robins from their original group had each claimed a tree for their home in a thick woods surrounding a clearing. A contented sigh escaped Cheeper's beak, and Lady gave an understanding chirp in reply. It was good to relax after the long months of flight and foraging.

Now, he and Lady were out exploring the countryside surrounding their new, southern home.

Cheeper

Swooping down over the countryside and then allowing the wind to snatch them aloft again, they drank in the sights. The effects of winter could be seen even here—dead grasses and barren trees—but it was certainly better than having to also deal with heavy snowstorms and a buried food supply. The poor chickadees, nuthatches, and juncos who had to weather the winter cold and snow back north didn't know what they were missing.

Cheeper and Lady coasted up and over a rolling hill, then down and past a narrow, paved road. They dipped down over the road, skimming just above a rough rail fence that lined the edge. Dry brown grasses waved in the breeze, and big, lumbering animals dotted the grassy field. Smooth, curving branches with pointy ends extended from the animals' head—the likes of which Cheeper had not even seen on trees.

Barren, dusty rows of furrowed earth extended far over the hills on the other side. Something had been growing there at one point, but now the field was hard-packed and empty. For a brief second Cheeper shut his eyes and tried to imagine what the landscape would have looked like if the meadow to the right had been filled with wild flowers and living, green grasses, and if the trees climbing the slope of a far-away bluff had been clothed in lush, green garments instead of standing naked and brown.

It would have been beautiful. If only…. If only…. Cheeper opened his eyes. It was just that, well, there had been something deep inside of him that had hoped that the death of the living things had only happened in the north, and that he would find again in the southern land the green, vibrant life he had once loved in his northern home.

Cheeper turned his gaze upwards as he and Lady glided around a bend in the road. The sky was a deep, azure blue overhead, and a filmy, lighter blue along the horizon. The sun shone just as bright and cheery-yellow in the sky here as it had in the north. Much, much brighter and warmer, in fact. For the first time in a long time, he and Lady were working up a sweat! Cheeper opened his beak and panted. A drink of cool water would have felt good right about then.

Yes, all was sunshine and happiness… on the outside. Inside… now that was a different story. Cheeper stole a glance at Lady, who was still eagerly drinking in the sights of their surroundings. This little feathered companion of his had something that he had not yet experienced: a genuine joy in her heart that did not depend on her outward circumstances.

The rolling hills leveled out into a flat plane, dotted with rugged scrub brush and brown, waving grass. Just up ahead was a cluster of buildings of varying sizes, surrounded by a number of scattered trees with spreading branches. Cheeper and Lady slowed their pace, holding their wings steady and allowing the breeze to float them higher into the air.

With Lady at his side, Cheeper circled high over the buildings, one large barn and three smaller sheds which attached to the fences surrounding the large fields. The white paint was peeling and roughened, but the frames looked solid and stable despite their age and the grounds were neat and tidy. A large, sturdy house on a rise a little distance from the other buildings reflected the sunlight in its many windows. There was something so beautiful about this well-cared-for farm. It was a feast for the eyes.

Unexpectedly, Lady uttered a little cry of delight. Following her gaze, Cheeper noticed the small glimmer of reflected sunlight in the front yard. Now, that couldn't be a window. It looked like a tiny puddle of water. Birds flitted to and from some feeders hanging from the bare branches of a tree nearby. They glided down for a closer look. There, supported a couple feet off the ground on a carved pedestal, was a large, stone bowl filled to the brim with water. Cheeper had never seen anything like it before. But it sure was convenient!

They fluttered down to the edge of the bowl and each took a long draught of water. Although slightly on the

86

stale side, the water did hit the spot. Their thirst quenched, Cheeper and Lady turned and, with cheeps of delight, splashed their wings and tails in the refreshing water.

Cheeper took a deep breath, stretched his wings, and yawned. Then he and Lady soared on the soft, southern breeze back to the tree in the nearby hills where they had made their home. His belly was full of worms and he hadn't a care in the world. The trip had been worth it. That night, Cheeper snuggled close to Lady on their branch, basking in her warmth as the temperatures dipped. They watched as the moon rose slowly, and Lady softly sang a nighttime lullaby. Life was good!

They returned to the farm often. They explored the roomy loft in the barn, drank and bathed in the stone water bowl, rested on the ridge of one of the small animal sheds, hunted for worms at the edge of one of the fields, and perched high in the branches overhanging the house. It was a peaceful, happy place to spend their time.

Occasionally, Lady invited other robins who also lived in their woods to join them. Once they had their fill of worms and anything else edible they could find, they often played together, hiding and searching for each other in nooks and crannies around the farm buildings or chasing each other back and forth from tree to tree. Other times they just sat around and chattered together. They were an energetic, exciting group, but Cheeper liked best those times when Lady and he could slip away to the farm all by themselves.

One blustery day, Cheeper and Lady and a few of her friends set off to while away the hours at the farm. The wind blew in chilly gusts and the sky was overcast with thick, gray clouds. Rain came in short bursts. Cheeper gazed over the dripping, dreary landscape. Things had been pretty when the sun was out, but the rain and clouds made the barren trees and ground stand out more than ever.

At least the rain made it easier to find the worms. They hunted worms between outbursts of rain. Again and again, Cheeper stabbed his beak into the soft, rain-soaked soil, nabbing a worm nearly every time. Some worms were wriggling through the muddy surface in plain sight, escaping out of the water-logged earth.

Another sheet of cold droplets showered down on them. Cheeper hurriedly hopped over to where the other robins were huddling on the ground next to one of the sheds. A slight overhang on the shed partially sheltered them from the chilling torrent.

Cheeper sat in silence, close beside Lady, watching as the downpour slowed to a drizzle, until only a few droplets pattered down here and there. Perhaps the sun would finally come out. Cheeper craned his neck to peer upwards at the sky. The clouds were just as thick as before. A stray raindrop struck him square on the forehead. A *cheep* escaped his beak, and he shook the water from his face. Apparently it wasn't quite done raining. Another minute or two under the overhang wouldn't hurt.

He settled back beside Lady and the other robins. Some twittered quietly together, some were silent. Cheeper closed his eyes. There was something so soothing about the *pitter, patter* of the gentle raindrops. It was putting him to sleep—

The atmosphere around him exploded. Cheeper's eyes shot open and involuntarily he launched himself into the air. He couldn't even see where he was going through the flapping wings and mass of robins' bodies that rushed past him in every direction. The screeches of fright were deafening. Something black and furry shot underneath Cheeper as he flapped upwards with the others.

Fear constricted Cheeper's chest. His breath came in short gasps. He sped for their home in the woods as fast as his wings would carry him. He couldn't see Lady and the other robins anymore. In their fright they had gotten separated.

Cheeper fluttered faster. The effort made his wings ache. He didn't have much energy left. If he could just make it back safely! He glanced over his shoulder again. He could just make out one of the slower robins falling further and further behind, his frightened cries growing fainter and fainter. He couldn't see the black... thing... anywhere. Perhaps it didn't have wings and couldn't pursue them.

Still, Cheeper pressed himself onward. He tore into the woods, twigs snapping and snagging his wings. It didn't look like they had been followed, but it was better to be on the safe side. Another quick glance revealed only the stillness of the woods behind him. Gasping for breath, Cheeper flopped down on the branch of his and Lady's tree.

Cheeper gazed around him, his heart pounding anxiously in his chest. The woods suggested nothing but calm. Leaves fluttered slightly in a light breeze. In the distance, he saw a couple of the other robins burst through the trees and collapse in the branches of their trees. Cheeper held his breath. Any second now the black monster would appear to terrorize them again.

A gust of wind shook the trees, causing droplets of water that had been clinging to the branches to sprinkle down on him. Far away he could hear birds singing. Cheeper released his breath and gulped the cool, misty air with relief. He was safe. His whole body shook with nervous excitement.

The straggling robin appeared, landing a couple trees over, gasping for breath. Any second now Lady would appear, sweeping through the clearing and settling beside him, frightened, but composed. Cheeper took another deep breath. His heart was finally slowing to a steady, rhythmic beat. What a scare that had been! Just what was that black creature that had attacked them without any warning?

The minutes ticked by. Lady had still not come flying back to him! Cheeper glanced nervously around. She should have been back by now. Sure, she had maybe taken a different route home, like the other robins, but how long would that have taken? Finally, Cheeper pushed off from his perch to make the trip back to the farm in search for his Lady. Hopefully nothing had happened to her.

Cheeper alighted on the bird bowl back at the farm not long after and scanned his surroundings carefully. The tree overhanging the house where they had often perched looked empty... the barn was quiet and still... the few scattered outbuildings.... There was the shed they had sat by during the rainstorm. But Lady was nowhere to be seen. The only living creature there was a sleek, black farm cat.

Cheeper's sharp eyes again scanned his surroundings. Where could she have gone? Perhaps she had tried to fly back to their tree home, only to get lost. But Lady wasn't a robin who got lost very easily.

Cheeper

Wait... there was something strange about the black cat crouching in the shadows of the farm shed. They had been attacked by a black creature just about that size. Cheeper's heart stopped cold in his chest. The cat was licking his chops and washing his face quite contentedly. Scattered at his feet lay a myriad of pretty feathers. Robin feathers.... Lady's feathers!

With a screech, Cheeper tore across the yard and flung himself at the animal, beating him with his wings and scratching at him with his feet. Cheeper eyes met the yellow eyes of the cat and saw them fill with surprise and sudden fear.

Fur flew as Cheeper scratched and pecked angrily. The cowardly cat turned tail and ran for the nearby barn. Cheeper pursued him only momentarily before turning around and heading to the place where all that remained of his beautiful Lady lay scattered on the ground.

Sorrow welled up within in his heart, and a mournful chirp escaped his beak. Lady was gone. Lady would never again fly by his side. She would never again cuddle next to him on chilly nights, chase him high upon the wind, or sing him to sleep with a sweet lullaby. Cheeper felt as if his tiny heart would break.

Cheeper sat in stunned silence there in the shadow of the farm shed. Minutes ticked by… maybe hours. He didn't know and he didn't care how long. Memories of his sweet Lady filtered through his mind one by one, each one bringing another pang to his heart.

Somehow he found his way back to the tree where he and Lady had been living. Lady's tree. The one that she had picked out because of the view of the clearing it offered. Never again would the two of them sit there together to watch the moon rise at night while Lady softly sang her goodnight lullabies.

Cheeper shuddered and closed his eyes to block out the thought. How was he supposed to go on living without Lady? Lady, who had taught him so much about surviving in the real world… who had been outgoing and encouraged him to come out of his shell… who gave him the courage to venture out of his comfort zone, explore new territories, and rise to new heights. Lady, whom he had relied on and, well, rather taken for granted. He could not live without her. He did not want to.

Hope

Cheeper struggled to beat his wings harder. Lady was calling him! He could hear her sweet voice trilling for him somewhere beyond the thick mass of dark storm clouds that blocked her from view. He was already using every ounce of his strength to propel himself out of the dark clouds closing in on him, suffocating him. He could not see where he was going—he only knew that he had to fly beyond the darkness to Lady. Far ahead, he could see sunbeams dancing beyond the wall of clouds, but he didn't have the strength to fly any further.

Cheeper found himself blinking slowly, awakening to the glitter of morning sunshine sparkling on the dew. From nearby trees came the happy songs of tiny feathered birds greeting each other and the new day. It had only been a dream, a horrible nightmare. And yet, it was more than a dream, too. It was as if he was trapped in a dense cloud of sorrow that blocked out the sun.

Cheeper

Of course, he could see the sunshine all around him. It brightened the whole valley and warmed his face. It was going to be a gorgeous day. Lady would have loved a day like this! If only she were here, she would have been singing her sweet songs and trilling to him in her pleasant voice. If only....

A couple of young birds raced past Cheeper's perch, screeching in delight at their merry chase. Just like he and Lady used to play. Was everything going to remind him of Lady? At the same time, did he really want to forget her?

Cheeper closed his eyes. Reality faded into the far distance as memory after memory engulfed him. Flying together in the warm sunshine.... Cuddling close to each other's warmth on a chilly evening.... Listening to her sweet songs.... It was as if he had no sunshine in his heart now, no warmth, no song. Not without Lady. She had been his song. He would just forget about life as it was now and live with her again in his thoughts.

His stomach growled. Cheeper groaned and opened his eyes again. So much for living in the past. When was the last time he had eaten anyway? Cheeper scratched his head with the claw of his foot. He actually couldn't remember. Oh, he certainly must have been finding food and water somewhere over the past few days, or he wouldn't still be alive. But he must have been doing so methodically—

almost as if another bird was controlling his movements—because he had no recollection of such actions.

He might as well head over to that muddy area in the underbrush at the edge of the clearing. Lady had discovered it, and there was usually always a worm or two in the soft soil. Sure enough, it didn't take Cheeper long to locate a juicy, wriggling worm. He sucked it down in a hurry and cocked his head to listen for another one.

All these worms were making him thirsty. Should he fly to the stream just over the hills on the right, or head over the hills to his left and go to the stone water bowl in the farmer's front yard? Cheeper hesitated. He hadn't been back to the farmyard since Lady had been… taken from him.

Spreading his wings, Cheeper took a running leap and hopped into flight. For some reason, instead of turning in the direction of the crystal clear creek that wound its way through the trees a few hills over, he found himself flying in the direction of the farmhouse where he and Lady had spent their last few moments together.

It wasn't long before Cheeper was sitting on the edge of the bird bowl, absently scooping up water. His eyes were on the little farm shed. There was the exact spot where he and Lady and the other robins had huddled together during the rain. The spot was empty.

Cheeper

Cheeper spread his wings and fluttered over to sit in the spot. Just what had happened after the cat attacked and they had all scattered? Had Lady tried to escape, or had she been frozen to the spot with fright? Maybe she had tried to fly away, but another robin had gotten in her way. If only he had checked to be sure she was following him! He had been so frightened, he hadn't even thought to make sure she had gotten away. He had just assumed....

Cheeper turned away and spread his wings. There was nothing in this place but heartache and unanswered questions. He had to get away from this place. For days now, it had felt as if his heart had died within him, and now he knew for certain that it was still very much alive—it was throbbing painfully in his constricted chest!

Bare trees and barren fields flew past below as Cheeper sped onward. If only his sorrows could be left behind just as easily. Why? Why did Lady have to die? Lady, with her sweet songs of praise to the Creator.

The Creator—if He truly was a God of love who cared for His creation, why would He have allowed Lady to die? First the brightly colored flowers had shriveled and died, the green grasses had been frozen by the frost and turned brown, the beautiful leaves had withered and fallen to their death, and now Lady too had perished! What kind of loving God would allow such death in His Creation?

Cheeper's restless thoughts wandered on. Until a faint sound reached his ears. Cheeper stopped his violent flapping and floated noiselessly along on the breeze, straining to hear the sound again. There it was! Cheeper turned and flapped in the direction of the sound, listening intently as it grew louder and louder.

Above the trees just ahead he could see a small, white spire reaching toward the sky. Then the woods thinned and parted, and in the clearing was white, high-peaked building which supported the spire. Shiny vehicles sat in neat rows off to one side, glinting in the sunlight. And borne towards him on the breeze was a lilting, beautiful melody, rising gently from the open windows of the secluded structure. Cheeper fluttered down and perched on the end of the high roof, hardly daring to breath for fear of missing one note.

The tune was very similar to the songs that Lady had sung. Where had he heard it before? Certainly not from any bird. He didn't understand all the words, but the music touched a chord in his heart. It spoke of the Creator—the God of love—sending His Son into the world to die for sinners. God's beloved Son… had died. And it wasn't an accident. His Son had chosen to die willingly to save sinners, whom He loved.

Cheeper

Cheeper's breath caught in his throat. Then God Himself had experienced the loss of Someone He loved! Could it be that He understood? Did this God of love care about the sorrow that rested so heavily on his heart?

The song ended and Cheeper winged his way back to the branches of his spreading oak tree. He gazed across the valley and the happy calls of the neighboring birds reached his ears. Of course, there were always birds singing and calling cheerily around him, but his own sorrow shut it out, like a thick storm cloud blocking out the sunshine.

He felt trapped. Trapped in sorrow and pain. Was there no escape? Would there never be sunshine in his life? He wanted the green grasses and beautiful flowers. The sunshine in a cloudless sky! He wanted the same peace and joy that had allowed Lady to sing her songs.

He wanted to sing. He wanted to be freed from the darkness of intense pain and deep sorrow that was taking over his heart and crowding out all hope and happiness. Lady would not have wanted that. Somehow, someway he had to propel past the clouds into the healing warmth of the sunshine! But how...?

For a moment Cheeper shut his eyes to the morning light, to the day, and to life. He couldn't go on like this anymore. He had to do something. Slowly, he opened his eyes, fighting to clear the haze and forcing himself to really look at his surroundings—not just glance over them, but to study them closely.

Trees spread out on either side and encircled the clearing. A few shriveled leaves still clung to some of the branches. Dried grass and scrub brush dotted the clearing, intermixed with piles of soggy, old leaves. The ground was damp and muddy in the open areas, where the sun had melted the frost that accumulated on an unusually chilly night. It was rather a bleak picture when he looked closely.

Yet, there was a certain charm to the day, as if nature had not given up all hope. The sun was smiling brightly down on the earth, the cheerful light flooding the shadowy corners of the valley. Wispy clouds floated lazily across the sky. Birds flitted here, there, and everywhere, their happy songs filling the air. Some were in groups and couples and some alone, but most had at least one friend.

Cheeper found himself gazing longingly at the birds who had companions. On a branch not far away, a brightly colored male bird landed near a brown-striped female and passed her a morsel of food he had found. A cluster of young birds was gathered under the trees, chattering away rapidly.

Cheeper sighed and looked away. Too bad he hadn't spent more time getting to know other birds like Lady had; perhaps he could have found comfort and encouragement in their companionship. Like Lady had done for him. Lady, with her sweet songs, cheerful spirit, caring heart... and troubled past. Strange, how she had always been the one to encourage him, when it was she who had gone through the most trouble in life. Why hadn't it been the other way around? Why hadn't he, whose life had been all sunshine and happiness ever since he could remember, been the one to comfort Lady, who had her own sorrows in life?

Cheeper shook his head, but he couldn't shake off the cobweb of tangled thoughts. He took a deep breath, filling his lungs with the cool morning air. It was refreshing.

Perhaps he was looking at it all wrong. Perhaps the fact that he needed the comfort and support of other birds wasn't as important as the fact that there were other birds out there that needed *his* comfort and support. Surely he wasn't the only bird who had experienced sorrow and hardship!

Yes, of course, why hadn't he ever thought of it before? Cheeper perked up on his branch as the insight struck him. Lady had experienced a sorrow very similar to his own, and yet she had found the strength to go on and even to reach out to others around her. Or maybe it was *through* reaching out to those around her that Lady found the strength to go on. If he could just be like her in a small way, perhaps he could also feel her joy. Could it be that this was his glimmer of hope, his ray of sunshine?

The prospect of another day didn't look so dull and dreary anymore. Cheeper began to comb through his feathers. He had been neglecting his appearance lately. Some of the feathers were dirty and dusty. He had totally forgotten to bathe when he was at the bird bowl earlier.... the same place where he and Lady had splashed and played on that fateful—no, he wasn't going to think of such things. He would fly over to the creek that meandered through the trees on the far side of the next hill over and take his bath. Feeling clean and kempt would certainly go a long way towards helping him feel ready for a fresh start.

The midday sunlight was growing quite warm, so the shadowy woods along the creek were cool and inviting. Cheeper splashed in the shallow water, ruffling and fluffing his feathers. Oh, did it ever feel good to get all the dirt out!

Cheeper

He stared at his quivering reflection in the rippling water. He was beginning to look and feel like a new bird already.

The days passed. Quite subtly, each new day now had a certain appeal to it. Who knew when Cheeper's opportunity to show compassion to a bird in need would come? His daily routine was now charged with expectancy. Whether he was bathing at the woodland stream or searching for worms and bugs, he was on the lookout.

When he took his midday siesta in the sunshine, he was careful to sleep with one eye open. As he exercised his wings in a flight around the "neighborhood," Cheeper kept his eyes sharply peeled to his surroundings. This time, it was not the thought of his own safety that inspired this alertness—instead Cheeper was watching and waiting for an opportunity to reach out to a robin-in-need.

Strangely enough, there didn't seem to be many needy robins around. Most of the birds he encountered throughout his day had mates with them, if not a whole group of friends. It was difficult to tell if they needed help or encouragement. He had almost been expecting to find birds all around him mourning in the broad daylight. No, birds weren't like that. They held their emotions inside of them, and it was rare to meet one that openly expressed its need.

So, how had Lady done it? Now that he thought about it, she hadn't encountered too many birds whom she had

104

known needed her help just because of their outward dejection. Most of the birds that Lady cheered and reached out to were ones that she knew and loved.

Like him, for instance. She had known when he was hurting, when he needed some encouragement or a song, because she was always with him. She knew him inside and out. She had been able to sense his feelings even when he did not display them outwardly. And all her friends... of course she had known their needs, because she knew *them*.

So, somehow he needed to become close to the other robins that lived in his part of the woods. He knew *about* nearly all of them—hadn't Lady been a friend to all of them and invited them to spend time with the two of them? But he didn't know them personally like Lady had. Somehow he had to work his way into their lives and hearts—not for the purpose of asking for their friendship, but to offer them his own.

It was a scary thought. It would be so much easier if he could just wait until he saw a bird who had an obvious, visible need, help them, and be on his way again. Friendship and love required commitment... sacrifice... the risk of pain and heartache....

It was a risk he would have to take. It was the only hope he had of filling the aching, empty void within. He would start slowly. Instead of keeping to himself and

105

moping, he would need to get out into the open and spend more time with the robins in his neighborhood. Best to start immediately.

Cheeper launched himself off his secluded branch and drifted down into the clearing. Several of Lady's robin friends were hunting for worms in the soft soil exposed between the scrub brush. Quietly Cheeper joined them. They were too busy calling to each other and holding competitions to see who could find the biggest worm to notice his presence. No matter—even if they took no notice of him, he would take notice of them.

Soon his quiet observance paid off. That smaller, scrawny robin had sidled over to the sidelines. Cheeper watched him more closely out of the corner of his eye. Sure enough: He was being left out of the trifling conversations among the other robins. He was being teased a little too much. Slowly and dejectedly, Scrawny Robin wandered away from the group, and none of the others seemed to miss him.

Cheeper hopped over to join him. He didn't know what to say, so he said nothing. Perhaps his presence alone would be enough. It was easier to hunt for worms in the solitude anyway. He could hear the swish of a huge worm just below the surface, and quickly tugged him out in the

106

open. What a find! Before he could even think, Cheeper hopped excitedly over to show the Scrawny Robin.

They both hunted in earnest now. Soon, Scrawny Robin had found a fat specimen just like Cheeper's, and was excitedly calling Cheeper over to see. They must have chanced upon a "nest" of underground crawlers. In their excitement, the two of them began happily calling and competing just as noisily as the other robins. Another robin heard their ruckus and joined them... then another.

Cheeper paused in midstride and gazed over the little group that had now congregated. Where there had been silence and sadness, there were now happy calls and friendly competition. It felt good. And he was actually enjoying himself. He hadn't had this much fun in a long time! With a happy *cheep*, he hurried over with the other robins to examine the extremely fat worm that Scrawny had found and was proudly displaying.

It became a daily routine. Cheeper joined the other robins in searching for worms and other food, always keeping his eyes open for any robins who might welcome his companionship. Soon he was joining in their games, and following them to their favorite haunts. He showed Scrawny to his favorite spot to drink and bathe along the winding creek. He showed a couple other robins the best places to find worms. The very things that Lady had once showed him long ago.

He found another friend, a soft-eyed, sleek-feathered robin with a cheery call. He and Scrawny invited this cheery robin to join them in exercising their wings around the neighborhood. He joined his new friends and other robin-acquaintances in exploring the far hills together. With calls of delight, they chased each other upwards until they could see a panorama of the countryside for miles around spread out before them. Then they zipped downwards at head-spinning speed to traverse a quiet, country road or follow a far-off river to its source.

They weren't a closed group—any robin was welcome to join them, especially anyone who was lonely. Cheeper met so many new robins in the weeks that followed that he couldn't keep track of them all. Happy robins, sad robins. Quiet robins, noisy robins. Robins with sorrowful pasts like his own. He would never have known that there were so many robins like him out there had he not resolved to open his heart to them.

On one of their excursions, they got caught in an unexpected thunderstorm that nearly frightened the feathers off Cheeper. They sheltered under the gable of an old, abandoned house. Cheeper jumped at another loud clap of thunder and glanced at the other robins. They all seemed to be taking the storm in stride. All except the normally soft-eyed, cheery robin. With a start, Cheeper realized that Cheer was shivering with fear, her pretty eyes glazed over.

Quickly, Cheeper pressed close to her, whispering encouragements and reassurances in her ear. It was as if she couldn't hear him at first, but he crooned on. Slowly her eyes cleared and her shaking disappeared. Still, she didn't fully relax until the booming thunder and pounding rain had finally subsided. Then her delicate eyes turned to him with a look of thankfulness that warmed his heart.

Then he had to shake his head at the irony of the situation: In his concern for his friend, he had forgotten all about being frightened himself!

Eventually, Cheeper even left his lonely spreading oak and joined the young robins who flocked together each night at the top of a tree. They huddled together in contented quiet to watch the moon rise, traded and "fought" over who was going to sleep in which branches in muffled, laughing twitters, sang goodnight songs, and whispered together long past their bedtime as only young robins can.

Cheeper sat staring up at the moon's soft glow and the twinkling stars even after the others had fallen asleep. His heart warmed as he reflected on the grateful glow in Cheer's eyes and the happiness that had replaced Scrawny's dejectedness. And then there were these young robins who had welcomed him into their hearts, and who had found a place in his own. His heart was full. He hadn't felt this good since... hmm... never before had he felt quite like this—even when he had Lady!

Lady.... Cheeper blinked slowly. He hadn't thought so much about her lately as he used to. Oh, he hadn't forgotten her. His days had just been so filled with thoughts of others that he had forgotten to sit and dwell on his own pain and suffering. It was not gone—only crowded away by the companionable, happy moments the past weeks had brought with his new friends.

There was something so satisfying about the thought that he was enriching the lives of others. Cheeper took a quick intake of breath at the thought that presented itself to him. In reality, *he* was the one being enriched! In reaching out to bless others, he himself had received a blessing!

Part IV
Spring

<u>Song</u>

Cheeper blinked slowly, stretched, and yawned. Soft, early morning whispers rose from the other robins in the tree. It was a pretty, delicate morning. Mist dripped off the tree branches and rays of orange sunlight streamed through the foggy morning air. Cheeper closed his eyes and allowed the sunshine to rest directly on his face. It was warm. He breathed deeply. The sun had already warmed the air considerably. He could tell that it was going to be an even warmer day than yesterday.

Well, it was about time to hunt out some breakfast. He and several of his friends rose from their perches and allowed a light breeze to float them softly over the landscape. What would it be? Bugs? Worms?

Cheeper focused on the landscape below. How brown and barren everything was! Of course, it had been that way for a long time now. He had almost gotten used to it, but now he awakened to it once more. How long ago had it been since he had seen colorful flowers, green leaves, and lush carpets of grass? It seemed like a lifetime.

Perhaps he would never again see them. He had been born just in time to catch the last few months of splendor before all the beauty in the world had died, never to rise again. Was he doomed to live in a world of dry, colorless death...?

Looking at it only reminded him of something that he had tried to forget. He still could not sing the songs of heartfelt praise that Lady had sung. Here he was, with scores of new friends around him, being blessed every day in putting them first, but, for some reason, he still did not have the genuine joy that Lady had possessed. It was as if there was a dry, barren patch hidden in his heart that mirrored the dry, barren world around him. Not even the best of friendships had caused this empty place within him to flourish.

With a start, Cheeper realized that the other robins were not in front of him anymore. He had to pay more attention! He had been so absorbed in thought he had almost flown right on past without noticing their decent. With a flick of his wings, he exited the current of air they had been riding and smoothly glided toward the ground behind the others. They'd hunt up some worms for breakfast. Lately there seemed to be more of them lurking near the surface of the ground. Perhaps the warm sunshine lured them up.

Cheeper poked around here and there, listening for worms only half-heartedly. He tried to join in the merry calls of his robin-friends, but finally gave up trying. He had been so happy these past few weeks, and now…. It was hard to admit, but it was true: There was still something missing.

Cheeper hopped forward and cocked his head to listen. It was almost tempting to consider forgetting everything and going back to his old, secluded way of life. Cheeper shook himself. That would never do!

He hopped forward quickly. He had been sitting there with his head cocked for several seconds, but hadn't even been listening to anything. He looked up and gazed at each of the robins who were hopping merrily over the turf all around him, searching for their breakfast. He would just have to try harder. To reach out more resolutely. To pour his heart and soul into caring for his newfound friends.

With this resolve, he pushed his troubled thoughts away and hurried forward to help a short, stocky robin pull a stubborn worm from the ground. After that he focused on listening for and actually hearing his own breakfast, as well as keeping up with and joining in the conversation of the other robins.

His eyes caught sight of the movement of a newly-hatched bug creeping along the ground. He scurried after the juicy morsel... and abruptly stopped short. There, almost hidden by the old, dead grasses, was a tiny blade of new, green grass pushing its way resolutely up out of the soil.

Could it be? What a sight for sore eyes! Cheeper almost hopped up and down in excitement, but instead he fixed a steady gaze on the ground, searching over every inch around him for more signs of new life. Yes, there was another one... and another!

Over the days, a sprinkling of green began to appear over the landscape. Tiny blades of green grass were springing up on the once-barren ground. Flowers began to bud, and tiny leaves unfurled on the trees. It was almost too good to be true. Cheeper stifled the spark that lit in his heart at the sight of the color and beauty springing to life. Best to not get his hopes up too soon. Perhaps it *was* too good to be true and would not last.

The days were beginning to grow longer again. The sun was beginning to beat a little too hotly on his back. He began to feel restless. Early one morning, in the gray light of dawn, Cheeper, Scrawny, Cheer, and other neighboring robins spread their wings and soared upwards, letting the warm south wind push them back towards their northern home.

This time, he passed the long days joining the fun with his friends, drawing closer to them every day. He was always ready to lend a listening ear if one of the robins needed a friend to talk to. He often took the lead of the whole flock, taking the brunt of any resistant winds while the other rode in his wake. He was quick to take responsibility to look out for dangers and places to eat and rest. It was the least he could do for these robins he had come to know and care for.

Still, there were times when the miles crept by below him and his heart ached for Lady. He missed their times of silent flight together, when they had enjoyed just being together without the need for conversation. He missed the swish of her wings by his side.

At these times the landscape slid past unnoticed. Cheeper's thoughts consumed his whole being. He was happy... at least on the outside. It was so satisfying to have friends by his side to care for and who cared about him. But there was *something* missing... he couldn't put his toe on what it was. And there was nothing he could do to fill the void. No, he needed something—or Someone—outside of himself to produce the genuine love and joy that Lady had possessed.

Could her joy have something to do with the Creator God whom her songs always praised? Maybe… but, no, that was impossible! The God of love who sent His Son to die for the human race could not be the same as the Creator. He couldn't love something as insignificant as a little robin.

Cheeper clenched his feet. If this God did love robins, why had He allowed Lady to die? Perhaps there was a God of love out there somewhere, but He obviously cared only for humans. But then… oh, well—it was all too complicated to understand! He just needed to forget about it…. If only he *could* forget about it!

Cheeper lost track of the days. Sometimes it seemed like they weren't making any progress at all! Yet, the air was definitely getting cooler with each mile they traveled, so they had to be making some headway northward. Eventually, he reached areas where the buds on the trees had barely begun to appear, and the grass was just turning green. Good thing he hadn't gotten his hopes up. What guarantee did he have that these signs of new life would last?

They often stopped their travels and camped in an area with a desirable food supply. At many of these places, another robin or two left the group as they found a place to make their new home or returned to an old home. It was difficult to say goodbye—more difficult than Cheeper had expected. He hadn't realized just how much his heart had become entwined with the hearts of Scrawny and these other special friends. At least he still had Cheer and a couple other robins with him.

Many of the places where his friends decided to stay were perfect havens for a robin, and yet, for some reason he couldn't bring himself to settle there with them. Maybe he was crazy, but somehow he knew that he had to keep going. Where to, he didn't know. Just that he was not yet reached his destination. But he would certainly miss each one of the robins he had come to know and love.

The sun's course was slowly angling northward. The weather became warmer and warmer. When the robins had first begun their journey back north, the weather had gotten colder and colder the farther they went. Now the southern warmth was catching up with them. Cheeper, Cheer, and their two friends had no trouble finding worms anymore. Still, they kept traveling, the other three for Cheeper's sake. He did not really know where he was going, but was heading somewhere.

Finally, for the sake of his friends, Cheeper settled down with them along the bank of a long, snaking river. Here there was an unending supply of worms in the soft soil of the riverbank. The trees provided shade from the sun, and the winds that wafted over the water were cool and refreshing. Cheeper, Cheer, and their friends could zip down over the river to catch bugs that lived in the cool rocks along the water's edge.

Still, it wasn't home. Cheeper felt this keenly. But he couldn't keep pushing his friends onward and onward. Besides, there was something familiar about this river, whose dark water shimmered through the trees that crowded closely around it. The more he thought about it, the more familiar it seemed. Had he been here before?

One day, he caught a swift current of air above the treetops and followed the river to see where it led. He had only rounded a couple bends when he came upon a solid-looking structure spanning the water. It was built of huge slabs of flat, white rock and was held above the water by corroded, metal pillars. A noisy vehicle flew past across the structure, making it from the one riverbank to the other without ever touching the water.

Cheeper was intrigued, and turned to follow the course the car had taken. He had barely begun following the dark-colored road when a winding, gravel road caught his attention. This road looked even more familiar than the river had. He had to see where it led! Down and around, past a little meadow of waving grasses and stubby pines. Around another curve. Up ahead, that sturdy tree with its thin sprinkling of baby leaves looked like the perfect place

Cheeper

for a robin to rest his wings.

Cheeper sank down on a branch with a contented sigh. Just below, a little creek trickled by and meandered underneath the road through a tunnel of tarnished metal. Something about the soothing sound of the gurgling water brought a refreshing peace to his heart.

This was a place where he could settle! This felt like home! And it wasn't even that far from the river where his friends were. Perhaps Cheer could even be persuaded to come here with him. They could build a nest in this very tree and raise a family of robins together. Cheeper liked to think that it wouldn't take too much persuading to get his soft-eyed friend to make her home with him.

Cheep-er, cheep-er, he chirped contentedly to himself, taking in the landscape before him. He took a

120

second look. What was it about this place? It looked so familiar! His eyes traveled carefully over every detail. The thin strip of woods bordering the creek… the gravel road… and that blue house up on the hill. Had he seen it before? Voices below turned his attention downward.

"Here, Sarah, let me help you rake this row smooth. We'll plant peas in here." A motherly looking woman picked up a rake and joined a young girl in a large rectangle of overturned soil. What an excellent place to look for worms! But those two humans…. Cheeper studied them intently. Surely he had seen them before—but, no, it was probably his imagination.

Cheeper again turned his gaze to his surroundings. The beauties of springtime met his eyes wherever he looked. All around him tiny, green leaves and grasses were springing forth, and there were even tiny, colorful flowers beginning to bud beside the blue house. So, the death of the creation had not lasted forever after all! From the barren ground and fallen leaves had sprung new life. Cheeper drank in the sights. Could it be that God's Son had not stayed dead, but had also risen to new life again?

Maybe, just as the beauty of summer faded into the death of autumn, so God's Son had to lay down His life in order to save sinners and wash them whiter than the snow that blanketed the barrenness of winter. But Cheeper was sure now that He had not stayed dead! Just as the bleakness and sorrow of winter gave way to the new life of spring, even so the Son of God must have conquered death and risen to provide new life for the humans who trusted Him.

What love! A light breeze ruffled his feathers, and laughter from the two workers below reached his ears. Cheeper furrowed his brow. There was no way he could understand such love. Would he be willing to die for his friends, much as he loved them?

God's Son had died for those who didn't even love Him. This was the type of selfless love that he needed in his heart. It was the type of love that Lady must have had. It was no use to try to find peace, joy, and love within his own heart. No friendship, no effort to put others first—not even the returning beauties of spring—could erase the barrenness in his heart.

No, Lady's joy and unselfish love must have come from elsewhere. And there was only one source of such love that Cheeper knew—the God of love. But didn't this God of love care only for human beings? Was there any chance that He was the Creator and life-giver of the animal and plant world as well? Could it be that He cared for the birds... for him?

A new sound caught Cheeper's attention. He cocked his head and listened. Drifting up from the two forms at

work in the garden below came a lilting melody of song. Cheeper craned his neck to catch the words. They spoke of the Creator God… of a tiny, insignificant bird falling to the ground… and of God seeing and caring.

Cheeper's heart beat wildly. Could it really be true? A tingle of excitement washed over him. It must be true! Then, the Creator *was* the God of love and cared even for the little birdies. An unspeakable joy welled up in Cheeper's heart. Then, God had seen when Lady died. He had cared!

Cheeper's joy overflowed and filled his entire body, every muscle in his body trembling with delight and awe. God cared for Lady, and God cared even for him, though he was selfish and undeserving! He could not contain His joy and excitement! He had to release it or he would burst! He opened his beak and out gushed a heartfelt, melodious song of praise which mingled with the melody of the two gardeners.

From that moment on, while his thoughts of Lady were still coupled with pain, Cheeper's memories of her began to be encompassed with happiness. He found a friend in every new robin he met. And now it was he who sang to them the sweet story of God's love.

"Look at the birds.... Your heavenly Father feeds them. And aren't you far more valuable to him than they are?" "God does not forget a single one of them.... So don't be afraid; you are more valuable to God than a whole flock of [birds]"

(Matthew 6:26; Luke 12:6, 7).

Postscript

I have had the privilege of being raised by my wonderful parents in the beautiful Minnesota countryside. I love living in the country—being awakened by the songs of the birds in the summer, feasting on the beautiful fall colors in autumn; sledding, skating, and cross-country skiing in the winter; and watching new life unfold in the spring. Living in the country, coupled with being homeschooled, has given me the opportunity to learn to do gardening, to raise puppies and kittens, to write and publish children's books, and to rescue and raise a baby orphaned robin.

  Maybe some of you are wondering why I chose to weave Cheeper's story the way I did—to have Lady die—

when I could have had it go in any number of directions. I wanted to tell a story about sorrow, because it comes to each and every one of us at some point in our lives. Though I have been incredibly blessed in my life, sorrow has still visited my family and me.

I am the youngest child in our family, and the only girl. I prayed for years when I was younger for a little brother or sister. Then, my parents made the announcement that in six months my dreams for a sibling would be a reality. I was ecstatic. But it wasn't to be. Miscarriage claimed (what I believe to be) my little sister, Aleicia Ann, only a month after. Heartbroken and confused, I was so tempted to doubt God and His love for me.

My mother was a great source of comfort to me during that time. Drawn together in our sorrow and disappointment, my mom and I became very close, and I began to turn to her for counsel and advice. This turned out to be my safekeeping through what could have been tumultuous teenage years. Thus, God brought good from what Satan meant for our hurt and pain. I may have lost my little sister (or brother), but I gained a friend in my mom. Not only that, but our whole family now looks forward to seeing Aleicia Ann (or perhaps Timothy Ken) when Jesus comes again. My family hasn't truly lost a member after all!

Cheeper

Friends, I can attest to the fact that God loves you—no matter who you are—and wants you to give your heart to Him. I am a witness to the fact that He can bring good from even the most heart-wrenching, sorrowful situations brought on by the powers of evil. I want the whole world to know that He can write His law of love on your heart, helping you to see those around you through His eyes. Won't you surrender to His love today? Won't you let Him change your heart and your life?

Other titles by Sarah E. Brown

Learning Lessons from Furry Friends will

introduce you to many of the Brown family's furry friends. Join the Brown family as they raise litters of kittens and puppies, experience hardships and losses, and turn every situation into a chance to learn valuable lessons about life and God. Learn about animals, learn about life, and most importantly, learn about the Bible and grow closer to Jesus by reading *Learning Lessons From Furry Friends.*

The Prodigal Pup is the

story of one dirty pup and one friendly missionary. The pup loves his master, but is torn between obeying him and doing what he thinks is fun. Then one day his fun gets him into a heap of trouble! Will his master rescue him? Sin and salvation. Repentance and forgiveness. Children will learn about these important biblical concepts through the fully illustrated, **TRUE** story of a naughty pup and a loving master in *The Prodigal Pup.*

Both titles are available in paper and e-book form from Amazon, Barnes & Noble, and TEACH Services, Inc.: 1-800-367-1844.

www.ingramcontent.com/pod-product-compliance
Lightning Source LLC
Chambersburg PA
CBHW072021060426
42449CB00033B/1600